Alan D. G. Oates.

THE SKILLS OF
THE ECONOMIST

by KENNETH E. BOULDING

> *A Reconstruction of Economics*
> *The Organizational Revolution*
> *Economic Analysis, third edition revised*
> *The Image*
> *Principles of Economic Policy*

THE SKILLS OF
THE ECONOMIST

BY KENNETH E. BOULDING
UNIVERSITY OF MICHIGAN

HOWARD ALLEN, INC., CLEVELAND

THE SKILLS OF THE ECONOMIST

FIRST PRINTING

Library of Congress Catalog Card Number: 57-13206

Manufactured in the United States of America

THIS ESSAY *originated in a series of lectures which I gave at the Fundaçao Getulio Vargas, in Rio de Janeiro, Brazil, in August and September, 1953. The lectures were published in a Portuguese translation in the* Revista de Economia Brazileira. *The first three chapters, now revised and brought up to date, appeared originally in* Contemporary Economic Problems, *published in 1953 by Case Institute of Technology.*

I take this opportunity to thank my Brazilian hosts, and especially Dr. Eugenio Gudin, at whose invitation these chapters were originally written. Seldom has a book been written in more agreeable circumstances, in a more beautiful environment, and never, I am sure, at the behest of kinder and more gracious hosts. I fear that the quality of the work cannot possibly come up to the quality of the experience which gave rise to it.

Nevertheless I hope that these chapters may be found useful and instructive. They are intended to give the reader some reflections on what economists are about in their busy professional lives, and what are the special skills to which they may lay claim. Most economists have felt an urge at some time in their lives to write a "scope and method"—not many are fortunate enough to find the time and place to do it. It may be complained that what I have written is mostly scope and not very much method. It may be that I have a better idea of where the land lies than how to get there! If however I can persuade the reader that economics is a serious subject, a genuine intellectual discipline, and a guidepost to problems even beyond its conventional boundaries, I shall be well satified. No previous knowledge of economics is assumed in this volume, though naturally those who are familiar with the subject will be better able to judge what I am talking about. I hope therefore that these chapters may be found useful by the beginning student who wants a foretaste of economics, by the lay reader who wants a taste of it, and even by the expert who may wish to sample what may be a slightly unusual bouquet.

Ann Arbor, Michigan
August 1957

Table of Contents

Economics Is What Economists Do

CHAPTER I

In modern thought, (if not in fact)
Nothing is that doesn't act,
So that is reckoned wisdom which
Describes the scratch but not the itch

MY PRINCIPAL OBJECTIVE in this essay is to examine some of the contributions which economics, as a distinct discipline, makes to the culture of our day. It is appropriate to begin by asking what economics is—which is really to ask what economists are. One recalls the famous remark attributed to Professor Jacob Viner that economics *is* what economists *do.* I therefore approach the contribution of economics by way of the skill of the economist, for if economists have anything to contribute to the culture of our time, it is through the employment of those special skills which have been developed in the study of economics.

These skills may be employed in fields remote from the actual subject matter of economics. This is one reason why I have chosen to emphasize the skill itself rather than the concrete subject matter from which the skill is derived. Skills developed in one area often carry over into other areas. A carpenter finds that some of his woodworking skills apply to metals; a pianist finds that some of his musical skill adapts itself to the violin. Similarly an economist may carry over part of his skill into other intellectual fields or even into the solution of practical problems of political or domestic life. It may be that Viner's definition of economics is too broad, for what economists do may carry them well outside the subject matter of economics proper and yet may still be done with their own peculiar skills. We should modify the Viner definition and say that economics is that study which develops the skill of the economist.

There is yet another reason, though a subtle one, for directing this inquiry toward skill rather than subject matter. The love of skill for its own sake is one of the most human of animal characteristics and one of the most civilized of human characteristics. The invention of sport is a clear testimony to the worship of skill. The drama of the baseball or football fields is not primarily of the mind or even of the emotions but of the intrinsic beauty of skill. On a more elevated plane the skill of the artist, the musician, the poet, the prophet and the saint are proper objects of human reverence. And somewhere between the baseball player and the saint it may not be inappropriate to study the skills of the politician, of the business man, of the union leader, and to make this study a principal foundation of social science. If we study the studier, and inquire into the inquirer, what better way also than to inquire into the nature of the inquirer's skill, and into the sources of his peculiar ability?

Before we examine the skill of the economist we should ask, "Who *are* the economists?" This is an embarrassing question. There are no recognized tests by which economists can be distinguished from those who may claim but who do not deserve the name. We have no professional qualifying examination as do the lawyers, the doctors, the accountants, and in some places, I understand, the beauticians. I know of no one who has been prevented from joining the American Economic Association or any other economic association for reasons of professional incompetence. We have no priesthood guarding the sacred fire handed down from Adam Smith. We do not even follow the practice of so many professions in improving their economic status by raising barriers to entrance. We may understand monopoly but we certainly do not practice it. Indeed, we are one of the few professions which deliberately, it would seem, attempts to undermine its economic status by actually encouraging students to enter it and by refusing to impose any professional standards.

Some unkind souls may want to deny us the status of a profession altogether. Morever, it is a common

3

belief that where two or three economists are gathered together there are always three or four varieties of economics present. We are popularly supposed to be divided by schools and racked by dissent, speaking with no common voice and being therefore quite unworthy of the name of science.

If these things be true it is an act of daring to claim there is a skill of the economist. Nevertheless, in spite of the divisions among us, and in spite of many signs of scientific immaturity, my experience with non-economists convinces me there is something, however humble, which can properly be called skill among those who recognize themselves as economists.

In anthropological language there is in the world a tribe, or a sub-culture, of economists, whose members recognize each other no matter where they live, whether in the United States, in Europe, in Australia, in India, or in South America. It is true of course that within this tribe there exist sub-sub-cultures—the Keynesians and the Institutionalists, the Neo-Manchesterians and the Economic Planners. This is not surprising. Within every tribe there are family quarrels and within any culture there are noticeable divergences. The homogeneity of a tribe or a culture must be judged by the nature of the internal quarrels, not their existence or even their intensity. Indeed, family quarrels are frequently the most intense of all conflicts because of the very closeness of the parties involved. And the quarrels of the economists *are* family quarrels.

4

As a more or less classical economist I may deplore the excesses of the historical school or the institutionalists but I must confess that I have learned a good deal from them. As a moderate Keynesian I deplore the ill-informed attacks of the extreme laissez-faire economists of the von Mises' school but I must also confess that some of the questions they raise are disturbing. As a firm believer in the virtues of the market economy I must even confess to certain virtues in the Socialist criticism and even if it is not quite true that we are all Socialists now (as a Conservative British politician said as long ago as 1880), at least those of us who are not Socialists have to look beyond socialism rather than before socialism and the most ardent advocate of capitalism has been more affected by the Socialist criticism than he perhaps realizes.

There is, alas, one sad exception to the happily familistic nature of the economists' quarrels. Between the Communist world and the West there is an almost impenetrable barrier across which virtually no communication takes place, even in the form of quarrels. Indeed, it is an essential feature of *family* quarrels that communication of some sort takes place between the contending parties. As a result of the quarrel there is at least interaction, some exchange of views, some modification of behavior. In some cultures family quarrels might almost be said to be part of the ritual of communication, and what to an outsider sounds like a small-scale war is in part an almost friendly argument— a fact

5

which becomes apparent immediately when the outsider tries to interfere and the family solidifies against his well-intentioned interference! It is a characteristic of true war, however, that it does not further communications and in so far as it modifies the positions of the contending parties, it drives them further apart or entrenches them in their original errors instead of bringing them closer together.

Such interaction as there is between the Communist world and the West is almost entirely warfare rather than communication. The Communist impact drives the West further toward a pure capitalism; the western impact closes the communist mind on the dry kernel of its dogma. There is a grim contrast between the closed and completely unfruitful relations between economists in the West and their counterparts in the Communist world and the relatively free and fruitful interaction of different schools of economic thought in the West. This very contrast, however, makes all the more apparent the fact that in the West there is a true scientific culture of economics characterized by constant communication, interaction, convergence of ideas, and development, as opposed to the large area in the Communist world where the scientific freedom has been suppressed in favor of a priestly orthodoxy, conformity to a party line, mealy-mouthed adulation of a half-deified leader and a half-deified body of "Scripture," and a ruthless suppression of any threat to the dominant power or the dominant ideology. Things are a little better since the death of Stalin but in spite of improved communications in some areas there has been little change as far as economics is concerned. As far as I know no western economist has yet been invited to lecture in Moscow nor does any reciprocal invitation seem in the offing. Economics was one of the first sciences to fall at the hands of the totalitarian economy. It is not wholly surprising to the economist to find that many other sciences—genetics, physiology, geology and now statistics—have shared its fate.

Enough now of justification. If I am to persuade my readers that there is indeed a skill of the economist I must at least try to explain what that skill is. The mere description of a skill, however, is a difficult matter. Ask the ball player how he manages to hit the ball and he will not waste time in words but will grab the bat and say, "Like this." A physiologist or a psychologist might, of course, have a different (and more verbose) view of the matter. However lengthy their explanations they would be incapable of transmitting the skill verbally. It is of very little use to a ball player to know with his mind what muscles make what motion for the skill itself is in the muscles and in the non-verbal part of his total organism. There is no substitute for the simple demonstration and really no way of learning but by trying, and failing, and trying again until the skill is built into the organism.

Our intellectual skills, likewise, have something of this muscular quality. They too, in a smaller degree,

7

are products of the whole organism so that it is not enough to think with our heads and our tongues—we must also think with our bowels! This is why one often finds students who know all the right words, who can pass examinations, but have no feeling for the subject. The skill has not *nucleated* into an organic whole. The student plays all the time with pieces which never form a pattern, the place and purpose of which he never quite sees. One cannot, however, help him much by *describing* the skill which he is supposed to have even though once acquired he may say, "Why didn't you tell me these things before?"—to which the only answer is, "I did!"

What follows, then, must not be interpreted as an adequate description of skills which cannot in fact be described but can only be acquired. Nor is it a short cut to the acquisition of these skills for those who do not possess them. It is merely an attempt to describe, as it were, from the outside what an economist does, just as one might say that a joiner makes furniture or an artist paints pictures. In these terms, then, one can say that the skill of the economist is that which is acquired in studying economic systems and in working with them just as the skill of the carpenter is acquired by "studying" and working with wood. We are thus thrust back somewhat upon the subject-matter again, since we must ask what an economic system is. Indeed, perhaps we should go farther and ask what a *system* is.

All skill relates to a "system" of some sort, that is, to

8

a coherent set of quantities, properties, and relationships abstracted, for the purpose of exercising the skill itself, from the immense complexity of the real world around us. It is important to realize that the exercise of *any* skill depends on the ability to create an abstract system of some kind out of the totality of the world around us. For instance, the carpenter is not interested in wood as a biological or chemical entity. He is sensitive to many of its grosser physical properties but not to many subtler ones. The wood of a carpenter is not the real—that is, the complete substance—but merely wood as a material on which the carpenter can exercise his skill. The point was illustrated nicely in a cartoon in the *New Yorker* which showed two lady baseball players in the middle of the field in animated conversation, the caption reading, "In the box behind me, a little to the left. A salt-and-pepper tweed with matching scarf that's really a dream." The skill of the baseball player is related to an abstract system of rules and properties of the physical and social universe around him and it is precisely the violation of the abstraction which makes the joke (if it is) funny.

In a similar way the skill of the economist depends on his ability to abstract a system from the complex social and physical world around him. The basis of the economist's system is the notion of a commodity. The economist sees the world not as men and things, but as commodities, and it is precisely in this abstraction that his peculiar skill resides. A commodity is anything

9

scarce, that is; in order to get more of it a quantity of some other commodity must be relinquished.

Scarcity is most obviously manifested in the institution of exchange where one commodity is given up and another acquired by one party and the first commodity is acquired and the second given up by the other party. Exchange, however, is not the only manifestation of scarcity. There are economic systems, like that of Robinson Crusoe, in which there is no exchange in the literal sense of the word. Nevertheless, there is scarcity in the sense that Crusoe's resources of time and energy are limited and therefore the various commodities acquire a value in substitution—what economists generally call *alternative cost.* Thus, if Crusoe wishes to build a house he must do without the things he might have acquired, or might have enjoyed, with the time spent in building the house. In this sense his house might be *worth* so many fish, or so many coconuts, or so many hours of dreaming in the sun which he had to give up in order to build it. From his point of view this alternative cost is a form of exchange, almost as if he had bought the house from someone else with fish or coconuts.

Similarly it is not difficult to see that all production is essentially a form of transformation of commodities akin to exchange. The miller exchanges flour for wheat by grinding it. The milkman exchanges milk-in-the-dairy for another commodity, milk-in-the-house, by transporting it from the dairy to the doorstep. It is not too much to claim that the phenomenon of exchange is

10

at the heart of the economist's abstraction and the ability to recognize and analyze exchange constitutes the core of his skill.

An economic system, then, is a system of commodities which are exchanged (i.e., re-shuffled by their owners), produced (transformed from other commodities) and consumed (destroyed). If this process is to be continuous there must be a constant stream of some original commodity or commodities (factors of production) which then undergo the processes of transformation, exchange, and eventual consumption. The system can be regarded from various points of view along the scale from static to dynamic. A purely static snapshot of such a system would reveal various commodities in the possession of various organizations and owners. For each owner or organization a physical balance sheet can be made up listing the various commodities (assets) which he (or it) possesses or controls. Even at this stage the existence of a financial system as well as a system of physical commodities is apparent—debts, money, and securities as well as iron, steel, wheat and houses. These financial assets have the interesting property that they generally appear in at least two balance sheets—in one as a positive item and in another as a negative item. Thus a debt is a positive item in the balance of the creditor and a negative item in the balance sheet of the debtor. Debts and other financial instruments are, however, commodities in the sense that they are exchangeable for other things.

11

Even in taking a static snapshot of the system it is possible to observe a phenomenon akin to *pricing*. The various heterogeneous physical balance sheets can be reduced to homogeneous financial balance sheets by the process of *valuation*—which in essence means expressing each asset (positive or negative) in terms of some common denominator or *numeraire* by multiplying it by a *valuation coefficient*. Thus suppose, what is usual though not necessary, that the numeraire is money—let us say dollars. Suppose then that the valuation coefficient of wheat is $2.00 per bushel. Any quantity of wheat in bushels can then be expressed as a dollar value by multiplying it by the appropriate coefficient of valuation. Fifty bushels of wheat would thus appear as $100. When all the items of a physical balance sheet are similarly reduced to a single numeraire (dollars), the total can be summed (both positive and negative items) and the sum is the *net worth* of the individual or organization concerned.

We now let the system begin to move. A complex system of events is observed. Some assets are consumed, as food is eaten, clothes wear out, fuel is burned, houses decay. Some assets are being exchanged among various owners or organizations in the process of buying and selling. Some assets are being produced, partly by the consumption of other assets, partly by the use of labor, land, and equipment. The use of these things, incidentally, is not the same thing as their consumption. In a given time period we can observe a universe of dynamic economic quantities: we observe amounts of commodity consumed, produced, transformed, exchanged, and the ratios of transformation (prices and costs) at which exchange and production transformations take place.

In the very simple model known as the stationary state or stationary equilibrium, (Schumpeter's "Circular Flow") all the balance sheet quantities continually reproduce themselves, like the trees of the forest, so that, even though there is constant change the whole system remains unchanged. Every time a commodity is consumed an equivalent amount is produced; every time a loan is paid back a new one is incurred. Both the human population and the population of all commodities and assets are in stationary equilibrium, with constant age distributions, births equal to deaths, and so on. This state of affairs is never found in reality though it has been approximated in some stationary societies.

In our society especially, the economic scene is continually changing. Populations of men and of things are constantly changing—usually growing, but some may be declining even in a generally advancing society as they are displaced by superior forms. Old processes and old commodities are constantly being displaced by new processes and new commodities. These changes frequently come in waves—one growth curve flattening off and then another coming along to accelerate the pace of change once more. The succession of growth curves gives the impression of cycles around the statistical trend. In addition to these apparent cycles there may be true cycles superimposed on the growth curves by certain dynamic instabilities of the system resulting, for instance, in a downward dip of the growth curves at the end of a growth period instead of a mere flattening off.

Such a system is immensely complex, and, if it is to be analyzed, various analytical devices and tricks must be used to reduce the intolerably complex mass even of this abstract system to manageable dimensions. In spite of the dynamic nature of the general system the most powerful tool which has been employed to date is still the idea of an *equilibrium* position of the various variables. This is a notion which can be employed usefully in varying degrees of looseness. It is an absolutely indispensable part of the toolbag of the economist and one which he can often contribute usefully to other sciences which are occasionally apt to get lost in the trackless exfoliations of purely dynamic systems.

The familiar equilibrium of demand and supply is the classical example of this method and it should not be despised even in a day of difference equations and linear programming. The equilibrium value of any economic variable, say the price of wheat, is that point at which there are no net forces making for change. If we may go beyond the strictly abstract world of commodities and recognize that they are in fact created, consumed, and exchanged by human beings, we may then say that, when an economic quantity is in equilibrium, no one who has the power to change it has the will and no one who has the will has the power.

Thus, in the competitive equilibrium of supply and demand, the price is such that the "market is cleared"— that is, the quantity offered for sale and the quantity offered for purchase are equal. Sellers would like a higher price, but, if one seller raises his price above the others he will sell nothing; if all sellers raise their prices together there will be excess supply—that is, the quantity offered will exceed the quantity demanded and some sellers will be left unsatisfied and, in a competitive market, will respond by lowering their price. Similarly buyers would like a lower price but do not have the power to lower it for a like reason. Even if they all lower their price together there will be unsatisfied buyers who will have both the power and the will to raise it again.

The equilibrium of demand and supply for a particular commodity can easily be generalized mathematically to the whole universe of commodities and we get the *general equilibrium systems* of Walras and Pareto. The ability to work with systems of general equilibrium is perhaps one of the most important skills of the economist—a skill which he shares with many other scientists, but in which he has perhaps a certain comparative advantage.

A general equilibrium system is one in which relationships exist among the variables so that only one, or a limited number, of sets of values of the variables is possible which satisfy *all* the relationships. The relationships are so defined that a failure to satisfy any one of them is either impossible (where the relationship is

15

a formal identity) or results in changes in one or more variables through the behavior of some person or other agency capable of affecting the variables. The latter type of relationship may be called a *behavior equation* because, if it is not satisfied, behavior ensues in the direction of an attempt to satisfy it. In a general system, with many equations and many unknowns, behavior which is directed towards satisfying one behavior equation is likely to result in upsetting certain other behavior relationships with secondary, tertiary, and even further levels of behavior resulting. Nevertheless, if the system is stable, a divergence from the position of general equilibrium (at which all the behavior equations are satisfied), must result in overall behavior which will eventually restore the equilibrium.

General equilibrium systems are of course met with in most, if not in all, sciences. The equations of motion of a solar system are one example; ecosystems in biology are another important example. The general principles of all such systems are essentially similar. A number of essential variables are selected. All possible identities relating these variables are formulated. Suppose there are m of these. Then n—m behavior equations relating the various identities are postulated. These behavior identities must be based on some empirically founded postulate regarding the behavior of the prime elements of the system. Such a system is called a *model*. It is clear that the building of models is not a purely mechanical process but requires skill of a high order—not

16

merely mathematical skill but a sensitivity to the relative importance of different factors and a critical, almost an artistic, faculty in the selection of behavior equations which are reasonable, tentative hypotheses in explaining the behavior of actual economies.

It is not enough, however, merely to set up a model with n equations and n unknowns. It is necessary to explore the *properties,* especially the dynamic properties of the model if it is to have any validity as an instrument of analysis or of prediction. Unfortunately, the more complex the model the more difficult it is to study its properties.

Three rather separate skills have been developed by economists to deal with this problem. The most general of these skills might be described as the method of plausible topology. We generally do not know the exact form of the behavior functions of our models. Nevertheless, we do know something about the general topological characteristics of these functions—i.e., their general shapes—even without extensive empirical investigation. Many of these topological assumptions can be derived from purely logical, or *reductio ad absurdum,* arguments. The famous *law of diminishing returns* is a good example. This, in any of its various forms, is an expression of the general topology of production or transformation functions of all kinds. In the case of the application of variable to fixed factors, the law can be demonstrated from the *reductio ad absurdum* argument that, if it were not true, we could grow all the world's food in a single flowerpot. Even in the somewhat more controversial form of eventually diminishing returns to scale, with all factors variable, certain *apriori* reasonings (e.g., the impossibility of making scale models of any organizational structure) are the foundations of the principle.

In certain other cases the topological assumptions about the nature of behavior functions are based on very broad general knowledge of human nature derived from introspection and non-quantitative observation. This is not to be despised as a source of valid knowledge, even in this day of econometrics and survey research. It is, after all, the kind of practical knowledge on which we depend in the conduct of our daily lives and in the innumerable small predictions in regard to human behavior on which all human interaction is based. When I stretch out my hand to an acquaintance I am in effect predicting that he will do the same and I am usually justified! The assumptions about the shape of demand and supply curves are, in large part, of the above nature. They are assumptions which have been abundantly confirmed in more quantitative, empirical research and even the exceptions to the general rules, in the shape of positively sloped demand curves for inferior goods, or backward sloping supply curves for individual labor, are very well understood and can easily be derived from equally plausible assumptions about the nature of preference functions. The assumed topology of the consumption function (relating consumption to income) in the Keynesian system is likewise an example of the method of plausible topology. It is not necessary to conduct elaborate empirical research to establish its validity as a first approximation regardless of how important second approximations, involving other variables, may turn out to be in the matter of economic forecasting.

The usefulness of graphical methods in economics is closely related to this method of plausible topology. The analysis of two or three variables graphs can express general assumptions about the topology of functions more simply than algebraic expressions. When it comes to the generalization of the analysis to more than three dimensions, graphic analysis tends to break down, whereas algebraic analysis does not, even though the weaknesses of conventional algebra persist. It may well be that the generalized topological analysis which mathematicians are now developing may turn out to be an important analytical tool for the economist.

The more variables a model contains the more difficult the task of exploring its properties. One of the most important skills of the economist, therefore, is that of *simplification of the model*. Two important methods of simplification have been developed by economists. One is the method of partial equilibrium analysis, generally associated with the name of Alfred Marshall and the other is the method of aggregation, associated with the name of John Maynard Keynes.

The partial equilibrium method consists essentially

19

in the exploration of cross-sections in two or three dimensions of the n-dimensional model. This is the real meaning of the *ceteris paribus* (other things being equal) assumption. We can illustrate again from the equilibrium of demand and supply. In the complete model we recognize that the quantity depends on many variables besides the price of the commodity concerned—for instance, on incomes and their distribution (which in turn depend on the quantities of other commodities and their prices), on prices of substitute or complementary commodities, on selling costs, or even on the weather or the political news. The quantity supplied similarly depends on a host of variables. Nevertheless, in order to explore the most significant properties of the general model, we assume all variables constant except the price and quantity of the particular commodity, and draw the familiar intersecting demand and supply curves to determine the equilibrium price. What we have done here is to cut the general n-dimensional figure with a plane in the price-quantity dimensions, going through the points in the other dimensions which correspond to the variables assumed constant. Having explored the properties of the model in this plane, we can now assume a change in one of the other variables, and in effect draw another plane across the model. Thus, by degrees, we explore its whole topology. We see therefore that the method of partial equilibrium is in no sense contradictory to the method of general equilibrium—it is, in fact, a method, and a highly successful method within limits, for exploring the properties of the general equilibrium models. Only if it is taken as an end in itself does it contradict the principles of general equilibrium.

Writers like Marshall and Wicksteed are skilled in the method of particular equilibrium but from them the student can often get a better notion of the properties of general equilibrium systems than he can by studying Walras' formal mathematical expositions of general equilibrium or even the empirical model-builders like Leontief or Lawrence Klein. By the time Wicksteed, for instance, has finished explaining how money contributed to a Chinese famine relief fund in England actually relieves famine in China, there is hardly a corner of the world that we have not explored. By then the student should have a fair idea of the immense ramifications of a general equilibrium model.

The second method for the simplification of general equilibrium models is the method of aggregation. This consists in adding and otherwise combining large masses of variables and treating the resultant aggregate as if it were a single homogeneous variable capable of entering into behavior equations which express in some measure the behavior of the whole aggregates in relation to one another. Thus if the particular equilibrium method consists essentially of *slicing* the n-dimensional model, the method of aggregation consists in *squashing* it—in compressing great complex chunks of n-space into a single line through the construction of indices of aggregates.

21

Instead of working with a thousand different quantities of output of a thousand different commodities, we make an index of output as a whole and use this as a single dimension in our model. This is the economics of the bludgeon rather than of the scalpel. Nevertheless it has an important place in the understanding of the gross dimensions and properties of the system. Furthermore it enables us to understand the mass phenomena of the system—such as mass unemployment, inflation or deflation—much better than the more refined methods of partial equilibrium analysis. It should be observed that the method of aggregation is not confined to economics. We resort to it constantly in other sciences and in daily life, whenever it is necessary to reduce a complex multidimensional mass of data to some unitary measure. When a professor grades a class, for instance, he is bludgeoning a complex mass of personality and achievement data into a simple (and misleading) linear scale of grades. Psychologists use the method constantly in the construction of tests, and even in the physical and biological sciences there is probably more aggregation of essentially heterogeneous data than is generally recognized. In economics however, the problems, the successes, and the failures of the method of aggregation show up with remarkable clarity. It is here perhaps the economist has a peculiar contribution to make.

The most striking example of both the success and the intrinsic difficulties of the method of aggregation is to be found in the simple Keynesian models. It is hardly too much to say that the understanding of the Keynesian model constitutes the difference between an almost total failure to comprehend the phenomena of mass unemployment and a reasonable understanding of its essential nature. It is a remarkable tribute to the power of the method that a model so crude and so full of faults should at the same time be so powerful in producing what might be called rough comprehension— and rough comprehension is infinitely better than no comprehension at all!

In its simplest form the model consists of only three relationships and three variables. The first is a basic identity: Production or Income $(Y) =$ Consumption (C) plus Accumulation (A). All that this states is that everything that is produced (created) in a given period must either have been consumed (destroyed) in that period or it must be still around somewhere! The second is a behavior equation, the consumption function, which states that aggregate consumption is a function of aggregate real income or production: $C = F_c (Y)$. The third is another behavior equation, $A = A_w$, where A_w is that amount of accumulation, or investment, which the system is willing and able to "take". We can either suppose that A_w is given by other elements in the system, as yet unspecified, or we can suppose that A_w is also a function of Y (that is, that there is "induced investment")—the formal analysis is much the same in either case. There is a simple graphic solution of the system. Thus in Figure 1 the curve C expresses the consump-

23

tion function; adding A_w to this gives us the *total absorption function*, $C+A_w$, showing how much product

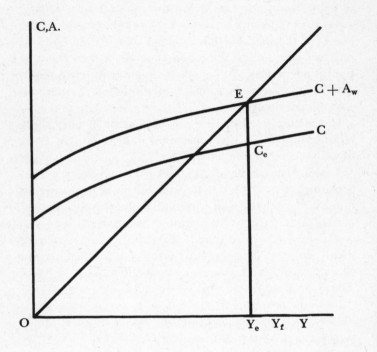

Figure 1.

would be willingly disposed of in consumption or willing accumulation at each level of income. The position of equilibrium is found by drawing the 45° line, OE, representing the identity $Y = C+A$, and finding where this line intersects the total absorption curve at E.

OY_e is the equilibrium output or income, Y_eC_e the consumption at that income, C_eE the desired and the actual accumulation. If output is greater than OY_e there will be unwanted accumulations which will cause cutbacks in output in order to try to reduce accumulation. If output is less than OY_e, there will be unwanted decumulations and output will be increased to fill the emptying pipelines.

The significance of the model, from the point of view of the theory of employment, lies in the fact that there is nothing in the model to indicate that the equilibrium level of output is in fact the full employment or the optimum level, however that may be defined. This full employment output may be at OY_f, in which case the system will exhibit an under-employment equilibrium. This will be the case if the behavior functions of the system are such that at full employment or optimum output consumption and willing accumulation is not sufficient to absorb the total output. There would therefore be unwanted accumulations, which, by various mechanisms, directly or indirectly, will produce declines in output and income. Unemployment is thus seen to be a response of the system to unwanted accumulations. It is the only response which a system can make to this situation, where the consumption function is stable, so that the unwanted accumulations cannot be dealt with

25

by raising consumption. Only by reducing output, in these circumstances, can the gap between consumption and income be reduced to the point where the accumulation is manageable.

The predictive power of this model is not very great, as the debacle of the Keynesian predictors after World War II indicated. This is because of the instability in the consumption and investment functions. Those functions which described very well the experience of the 1930's did not apply very well to the 1940's. This apparent instability may, of course, be the result of *over aggregation,* which is always one of the potential weaknesses of the aggregative method. It may be, for instance, that the composition and distribution of income is an important element in the determination of consumption patterns so that with the same aggregate income of different compositions consumption might be different. Also there may be other important variables in the system which do not get into the model at all. These may affect the height of the consumption function—that is, the amount consumed at each level of income. The total stock of capital, the total stock of money, the rate of interest, and the highest level of past income are a few of the many variables which have been suggested as relevant to an extended consumption function.

In spite of its weak predictive power, however, the *interpretative* power of the elementary model is substantial. It throws a great deal of light on what should be or should not be done in a situation of unemployment. Thus it is clear that, if there is an underemployment equilibrium as in Figure 1, there are two principal roads to full employment. One is to raise the consumption function and the other is to raise the investment function so that at each level of income more will be consumed and willingly accumulated than before. This is the rationale of such devices as an easy money policy to stimulate investment, or a budget deficit policy to increase liquidity and so raise both the investment and the consumption functions. One must always be on the lookout for secondary psychological effects. Thus a policy which might have a direct effect in encouraging investment might, at the same time, create a climate of business opinon which will discourage investment. It is something, however, to know the direction of the direct effects and on the whole a thorough understanding of the simplest aggregative models will increase this knowledge substantially. We can at least be spared the spectacle of a government trying to cure unemployment by increasing taxes, running a budget surplus, cutting expenditures, and raising interest rates!

There are two areas I have not yet mentioned in which the economist can claim some special skill. These are the two pillars of Samuelson's *Foundations of Economic Analysis*. The first is the theory of maximization, or more generally, the theory of rational behavior. The second is the theory of difference equations, or of dynamic processes.

27

In the course of his pursuit of the laws which govern the universe of commodities, it has proved to be impossible for the economist to insulate himself altogether from the world of human and organizational behavior. Consequently the economist has developed an elaborate theory of *economic behavior,* based on the simple assumption that the individual maximizes something, something which is a function of the set of variables which are relevant to the individual's economic position and some of which are under his control. This theory is known as the *marginal analysis.* In the case of the firm the maximand is generally assumed to be some measure of financial profits. In the case of the household an abstract preference-quantity known as *utility* is supposed to be maximized, though, as I hope to show, the assumption of profit maximization in the case of the firm is a highly special case, valid only under certain conditions. Even in the case of the firm it must generally be assumed that "utility" is maximized.

This theory of behavior is far removed from those based on stimulus and response patterns in psychology or on crisis and adjustment patterns in sociology. The economist is not much of an economic man when it comes to borrowing from other sciences. Generally speaking, if, in the pursuit of the world of commodities he stumbles into the world of men, he prefers to make up his own psychology on the spot rather than borrow from the psychologists. The psychologists, not unnaturally, are somewhat critical of this insular behavior.

Nevertheless, once it is understood that the economist's interest is not human behavior but the behavior of commodities then his development of something as psychologically peculiar as the marginal analysis takes on more meaning. The core of the economist's interest is not human behavior as such but the *behavior functions* which relate his economic quantities, his prices, and his quantities of commodity produced, consumed, or exchanged. The marginal analysis has retained the interest of the economist because it seems to yield as a *conclusion* the assumptions about behavior functions which are the *postulates* of economic analysis proper.

Any other behavior theory would be just as acceptable to the economist which yielded the same conclusions and helped answer the following type of question: "Do higher prices mean smaller purchases?", "Do higher wages mean smaller output?" The marginal analysis has provided what seemed to be a reasonable answer to these questions, or at least a rationale for obtaining those answers, and its long-continued popularity with the economists is undoubtedly related to the failure of substitute theories of behavior to provide any answers at all. It is possible, as I shall indicate later, that we are on the verge of developing better and more relevant theories of behavior. The economist will not give up the marginal analysis, however, until something emerges which is clearly of more use to him for his special purposes.

In spite of all the space given to it in the textbooks

29

of economics the marginal analysis appears to be more of a front porch than an integral part of the edifice of economics. It is a large and imposing porch trimmed with fine arches and handsome diagrams but it could be torn down and a different structure erected without seriously affecting the main building.

If the marginal analysis is a front porch, process analysis is perhaps the back porch—something which has been developed by economists but which clearly leads into other fields and other uses. If we know exactly how tomorrow is related to today we can obviously proceed to an indefinite series of tomorrows. Tuesday can be derived from Monday, and now having got Tuesday we can derive Wednesday, and from Wednesday, Thursday, and so on to the Day of Judgment. The astronomers got there with this game long before the economist and one wonders how possible it will be to find stable relationships of this sort (i.e., difference equations) in the social sciences. It is certainly worth trying, and the predictive power of economics, like that of any other science, depends on its ability to find stable difference equations within its universe of variables. However, skill in the analysis of these dynamic processes is not peculiar to the economist. It is something he must share with many other sciences.

Perhaps the best way to test the skill of the economist is to put him in the position of Economic Adviser to the Philosopher King (or President!). If he has any skill at all it will soon be revealed. One needs, of course, a proper humility. There are a great many questions on which the economic adviser cannot presume to give advice, even fundamental questions regarding the most desirable structure of the economic system, or relatively trivial questions about a tariff on buttons. Also there are a great many economic questions which are bound up with matters of peace and war, with the retention of power and the satisfaction of political obligations, with social justice and the racial or cultural stratifications of society, in which the economist has no special competence.

When, however, it comes to the question of what to do about a depression or an inflation, whether price control can be applied without rationing, what sort of public finance leads to inflation, and even on some of the more obvious conditions of economic development, the economist has something to say by virtue of his peculiar skills even if only to give a sense of direction. And if one compares the kind of answers and understanding which the economist is able to give to the question, for instance, of how we avoid or get out of a depression, with the kind of professional answers that the political scientist might give when asked what policies decrease the possibility of war, or the answers a sociologist might give to the question of what policies promote happy families or good race relations, the economist may at least be pardoned a touch of the disagreeable pride that comes from odious comparison.

A Universe of Commodities

CHAPTER II

Economists are understood
To study goods, if not the Good
Although their goods, we often find
Are pale obstructions of the mind

I HAVE ARGUED that the skill of the economist lies in the analysis of the behavior of commodities and not the behavior of men. It is not altogether surprising therefore that in spite of the apparently close relationship between their subject matters, the main contributions of the social sciences to the conduct of business have not come from economics but from the more "behavioral sciences" of psychology and sociology. Human relations, industrial relations, public relations, group dynamics, even the psychology of advertising, have all made substantial contributions to the business vocabulary.

The world of the economist and the world of the

business man, however, have shown small signs of coming together in spite of the fact that economists have spent a great deal of time and effort in developing an elaborate theory of the firm. The vocabulary of the economist seems quite foreign to the man of affairs; all this talk about equating marginal this to marginal that is so much academic gibberish to the great fraternity of "those who have to meet payrolls." Nor on the other hand have the students of management—even the academic students of management—been able to communicate fruitfully with the theoretical economists. The collection of organization charts, platitudes, and maxims which characterize the average textbook on management fills the economist with unrestrained ennui because there is so little relationship to the problems which strike the economist as important.

In part, this unfortunate situation arises because of a difference in point of view. The economist's focus of interest, I must repeat, lies in the world of commodities and not in the world of men. Hence the actual problems of the organization and conduct of business, which are problems in the relations of men rather than in the relations of commodities, do fall more naturally into the realm of the psychologist and the sociologist rather than that of the economist in spite of the traditional association of business with economics.

But I must also regard this persistent inability of economists and business to communicate as unfortunate. On the one hand the economist cannot wholly under-

33

stand the laws which govern the universe of commodities without knowing something about what governs the universe of men. On the other hand business men do have something to learn from economists, even if it is only from his way of looking at things and at their businesses, which may increase their understanding of what they are doing even if it does not increase their skill. Moreover, recent developments in economics indicate that in the not too distant future economists may have something of great importance to contribute to the theory and practice of the business enterprise as well as other organizations.

Ten years ago I would have said that the marginal analysis, or the theory of maximization, was the only contribution of economics to the theory of the business enterprise. This is no longer true and it is becoming clear that the marginal analysis, as we understood it ten years ago, is a special case of a much more general theory, not only of a more general theory of maximization, as expressed for instance in the theories of linear programming, but also of a more general theory of behavior and organization. Nevertheless, for the purposes of the present argument I propose to neglect much of the work of the past ten years and consider the possible contributions of the marginal analysis as it is conventionally understood.

The marginal analysis is nothing more nor less than the detailed spelling-out of the theory of maximization— that is, the theory that *optimum* position of the variables

34

of any economic organization is that given by the maximum position of that variable which measures desirability or preference. The first basic assumption is that any economic organization is characterized by a set of identifiable variables—prices, quantities, selling costs, and so on—and that these variables are linked in a series of transformation functions which set the *limits* to the possible combinations of the variables. The principal transformation functions are (i) the production function, which reflects the limitations imposed by the nature of the physical world on the amounts of outputs which can be got from specific quantities of inputs, and (ii) the sale and purchase functions which show what quantities of sales of output or of purchase of input are consistent with various prices, selling costs, etc. What these transformation functions do is to delimit the set of *possible* combinations of variables: any set which does not satisfy the limitations laid down by the transformation functions is by definition impossible of attainment. It is not enough, however, to delineate the possible, for even with man a great many combinations are possible, though not all things. Within the range of the possible we need a method of identifying the *optimum* set of variables. To do this we postulate that some quantity, which is a function of all the other variables, is a measure of desirability so that any set of variables or position of the organization for which this desirability-measure is higher is *ipso facto* better than a set or position for which the desirability-measure is lower. The

35

bigger the desirability-measure, the better! Then clearly that position of the system (that is, that set of values of all the relevant variables), at which the desirability-measure is a maximum, is the "best."

All this sounds very abstract, but I will illustrate with a very simple case—perhaps the simplest possible case—of an economic organization. Suppose we have a firm which is engaged solely in the business of buying and selling a single commodity—say wheat. We will suppose that the assets of the firm consist of two items only—wheat and money. We will further assume a perfect market for wheat—that is, that the firm can buy or sell as much as it likes at a given market price but that if it raises its price above the market it will not be able to sell and if it lowers its price below the market price it will not be able to buy. Then suppose we plot quantity of wheat on one axis (OW) and quantity of money on the other (OM) as in Figure 2. Then any actual position of the firm can be represented by a point in this field, say T, where KT is the amount of money and HT is the amount of wheat which the firm possesses. The transformation function (or "opportunity line" as it is often called) is the line MTW—the slope of which is equal to the market price of wheat. A movement up this line in the direction of M indicates that the firm ·is selling wheat and "buying" money: a movement towards W indicates that the firm is buying wheat and "selling" money. The price of wheat is the slope of the line, OM/OW.

We now take the line MW and make it the horizontal axis of Figure 3, the vertical axis now being the desirability or advantage-measure, which I have labeled, following the conventional terminology of economics, "Utility". Utility is a maximum at X and the corresponding position of the firm, L, is therefore the optimum. Each position in the line MW represents a possible combination of wheat and money but only L is the "best." Measuring ML on Figure 2 equal to ML

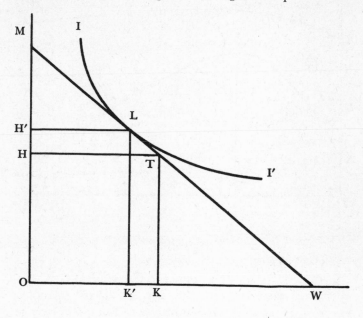

Figure 2.

on Figure 3 we see that the "best" amounts of wheat and money to hold are LH' and LK' respectively. At the maximum point X, and at no other, the *net marginal advantage*—i.e., the slope of the curve UXU'—is zero.

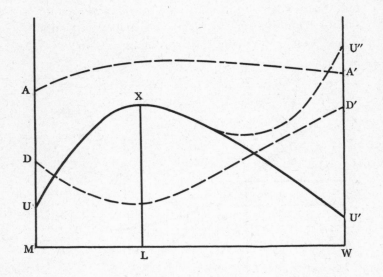

Figure 3.

We can, if we like, separate the gross advantage from the gross disadvantage—the net advantage being of course the excess of gross advantage over disadvantage. Then we can draw, in Figure 3, gross advantage and

38

disadvantage curves, AA' and DD'. Where the slopes of these curves are the same the net advantage (the vertical distance between them) is the greatest. That is to say, the optimum position is the marginal gross advantage equal to the marginal gross disadvantage.

The reader who is familiar with the marginal analysis will of course recognize the above equality as the general case of all the *marginal conditions*. If gross advantage is measured by revenue and disadvantage by cost, we get the familiar *marginal revenue equals marginal cost* condition for a maximum of net revenue at a point on the output axis, or the equally familiar *marginal revenue product equals marginal cost of input* at a point on the input axis. The final optimum is that combination of variables at which all the various marginal equalities are satisfied simultaneously. We recognize here both the principle of a general equilibrium model and the *method* of partial equilibrium outlined in the first chapter—for the ultimate position of the optimum can be found only by solving all the marginal equations simultaneously, yet it is useful to explore the topography of the model plane by plane.

A number of alternative methods are possible for describing the preference or advantage function. For instance, in Figure 2 we suppose that net advantage is measured in the vertical direction and an advantage-surface is drawn in three dimensions over the plane of the paper. This surface can be represented by a set of contours such as ILI', all points on which represent combinations of equal advantage. These are the familiar indifference curves of Pareto. The optimum point is that at which the opportunity line is *touched* by an indifference curve, for at any point on the opportunity line which is *cut* by an indifference curve it is possible to move to a more advantageous position, represented by a "higher" indifference curve. The point L, however, where the opportunity line is touched by an indifference curve represents the "highest" indifference curve, and therefore the most advantageous position possible while keeping to the opportunity line MW. It may be noted here that the opportunity line is in general a "boundary" rather than a line, in the sense that positions *within* the line are possible by throwing one or the other asset away. Thus, all positions downward and to the left of the opportunity line are possible of attainment; all positions upward and to the right are impossible of attainment.

In general, the transformation functions of all kinds may be thought of as boundaries which cannot be transgressed, rather than as tight ropes to be walked, separating the variable-space into two parts. One part includes all possible sets and another includes all impossible sets. In Figure 2 we can think of the opportunity line as a fence on the "mountain" of the advantage surface. The optimum possible point is the highest point on the fence, which is precisely where the fence touches a contour. There are points, of course, which are still higher up the advantage mountain but since they are on the other side of the fence they are not attainable.

40

I need not go into all the innumerable ramifications and developments of the essentially simple ideas expressed above. Enough of them will be found even in my own *Economic Analysis* and still more in my *Reconstruction of Economics* to satisfy the most avid thirster after this kind of knowledge. It will suffice here to say that exactly the same principle which I have outlined here can be applied to any and all the variables which are significant in the life of an economic organization, whether costs, inputs, outputs, selling costs, production functions, borrowings, lendings, inventories, capital structures or time structures. In all these cases the principle is the same. First, we postulate some sort of transformation or opportunity function which divides the possible from the impossible. Then we find, within the area of the possible, some technique for describing the most desirable. This may be the selection of one variable of the system, such as profits, as a unique measure of desirability. It may be by setting up a "utility" or advantage function in the form of indifference curves. Even simpler devices may be useful such as the one I have proposed in my *Reconstruction of Economics* expressing preferences in terms of preferred asset ratios. Whatever the application the essential principle is the same.

The main question I raise is why a system of analysis, so self-consistent, so obedient to the great scientific principle of parsimony, so elegant, so persistent in academic teaching, and so admirably adapted to the understanding of students and to regurgitation in examinations, should

41

be so confoundedly useless—useless, that is, to the business man who is supposed to be the prime mover of the whole apparatus. For the business man, alas, either finds the whole rigmarole so unfamiliar that he does not even attempt to master it, or if he does master it (and there are rare business men here and there who have done so) is apt to deny indignantly that he behaves in any such monstrous and outrageously unethical profit-seeking manner as the marginal analysis seems to suggest.

First we examine one or two technical defects in the marginal analysis as usually presented to see if these throw any light on the problem. First we have the problem of the "boundary maximum". Suppose, for instance, in Figure 3, that the net advantage curve, instead of falling continuously from X to U', first fell and then rose to U" where U" represents a higher level of advantage than X. Suppose further that the conditions of the problem preclude any position beyond W*.

---

*We may note in passing that in the example of Figures 2 and 3 the opportunity line may be extended into the fourth quadrant beyond W by borrowing money (in which the individual expands his wheat holdings beyond his net worth by acquiring, as it were, "negative money" in the form of debt). Similarly the line may be meaningfully extended into the second quadrant beyond M by "borrowing wheat" (selling wheat futures) and so increasing the money stock beyond the net worth.

Then U″ represents the true positon of maximum advantage, not X, though U″ fulfills none of the mathematical conditions for a maximum and none of the marginal equalities or conditions are satisfied. The marginal conditions merely represent a maximum "in the small": they may not represent the absolute maximum at all.

A variant of the same problem is presented when there are multiple maxima (dromedaries instead of camels) because the marginal conditions apply equally well at any of the maxima and throw no light on which of the various "humps" is the *maximum maximorum*.

Another variant of the same problem is that presented by discontinuities in the transformation functions. For many reasons these discontinuities can occur in almost all the transformation functions. They can occur in a sales function where a commodity has a number of distinct and non-competing uses at different prices, but where in any particular use below the price at which this use comes into play, the demand is highly inelastic. The sales curve for such a commodity (and the case is not infrequent, especially in raw material industries) will look more like a staircase than a nice smooth demand curve. The resulting discontinuities in the revenue curves are likely to yield advantage-functions with sharp jagged discontinuities, like a saw in profile. The marginal conditions will be formally satisfied even at such jagged peaks but not much in the way of conclusions can be drawn from the analysis except to say that the highest tooth of the saw is the best!

43

I shall do no more than mention the difficulty that the marginal conditions of the first order apply just as well to minima as to maxima since this is a problem which can be taken care of adequately by the second-order conditions. Indeed, a careful statement of the marginal conditions in a negative sense usually includes implicitly the second order conditions. Thus, in Figure 3 we might say that the advantage is at a maximum when the marginal advantage, with respect to increase of either commodity, passes from a positive to a negative value with increase in the quantity of the asset.

None of these difficulties in themselves are adequate to explain the deaf ears on which the marginal analysis falls in the business community. There is a deeper problem than any we have mentioned. It is the problem of *what* is maximized—that is, what is the measure of advantage and how is it measured. The answer the economist has usually given to this question, as far as the business enterprise is concerned, is that, considered in its abstract nature as an economic organization, the business should maximize profits. Two problems face us at this point. One is the measure of profit itself. The other is the persistent belief in the business community that a decent, respectable, or even merely cautious and conservative business man would not want to maximize profits even if he knew how to do so.

We will consider first the problem of the *measure* of profits. In the elementary marginal analysis, as it is usually taught in the first course in economics, it is assumed that profits are measured by the *net revenue*. This is the difference between the total revenue, or the value of the product, and the total cost, which consists essentially of the assets (including liquid assets) consumed or destroyed in the production of the product. The maximization of net revenue then gives us the "simple" marginal conditions, such as *marginal revenue equals marginal cost*. The net revenue is only a satisfactory measure of profits as long as we abstract from the time and capital structure of the enterprise. When we try to generalize the marginal analysis to cover the whole time and capital structure of the enterprise, as Friedrich and Vera Lutz have attempted to do, net revenue as a measure of profits must be replaced by some concept of a rate of return or net worth or capitalized value. Two enterprises with the same net revenue of, say, $10,000 a year, would not be regarded as equally profitable if one was capitalized at $100,000 and the other at $200,000. Similarly within a single enterprise the maximum net revenue might appear so "late" in time after the commencement of the enterprise that the rate of return on capital investment would be smaller than if the net revenue were smaller than its maximum but appeared earlier.

Even though it is clear that the net revenue is not an adequate measure of profits over time it is not so clear what should be substituted for it. The Lutzes list four contenders for the throne of the maximand, three of which are serious rivals although their claims are by no means fully resolved even within the fraternity of economists. These are: the rate of return on the total assets of the enterprise; the rate of return on the entrepreneurs' own capital; and the present value of all future net receipts capitalized at market rates of interest.

The idea of a *rate of return* and its relationship to the net worth or the capital value of an enterprise is so fundamental at this level of the theory of the firm that we may well pause for a moment to examine it. Let us consider first the nature of the profit-making process itself. The study of the *process* in this case is probably the best clue to the correct *measure*. Let us return to our simple example of the wheat firm and consider how such a skeleton firm can ever make profits. In order to understand the profits concept it is necessary to develop a concept of a financial balance sheet and a net worth. This can easily be done in the present case if we suppose that a valuation coefficient can be applied to the stock of wheat to reduce it to a dollar value. The dollar value of the wheat and the dollar value of the money would thus be added to form the net worth of the firm. This is shown in Figure 4 in which the axes are the same as in Figure 2. I assume that the value of the amount of wheat H'L is H'M', so that the net worth of the firm at the point L is OH' + H'M', or OM'. The valuation coefficient for what is the H'M'/H'L dollars per bushel. It will be noticed that I have assumed that the valuation coefficient is different from the market price. This is to emphasize the point that the two concepts are essentially separable, even though closely related.

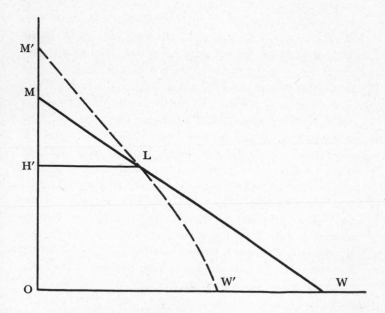

Figure 4.

In Figure 4 the valuation coefficient is greater than the market price (the slope of LM′ is greater than the slope of LM). Under these circumstances it is clear that the further the firm moves down towards W, or even beyond if possible, the larger its net worth. If the valuation coefficient had been less than the market price the reverse would have been true—a movement in the direction of M, or beyond, would increase the net worth. If the market price and the valuation coefficient are the same it is clear that no amount of movement along the opportunity line will change the net worth. It is fairly evident that no *maximizing of profit* procedure means anything when applied to a single act of buying and selling. If the valuation coefficient is equal to the market price no profits can be made by buying and selling, because, no matter how much is bought and sold, the net worth remains the same. If the valuation coefficient is not equal to the market price net worth can be increased by moving as far as possible in one direction or the other until either certain boundaries are reached through the inability to borrow money or wheat, or imperfection in the market makes the opportunity curve steeper as the holdings of wheat increases. In this case the maximum net worth is at that position where the valuation coefficient is equal to the (marginal) price of the commodity. Thus, suppose in Figure 4 that after the point L the market became imperfect and the firm could only acquire more wheat by paying higher and higher prices. The opportunity line would curve round as in LW'. If M'L were tangent to this curve LW' at L, it is evident from the geometry of the figure that OM' is a maximum net worth in the sense that further purchases of what beyond H'L would lower the net worth at the given valuation coefficient.

As long as we stick to a single transaction we shall not perceive the essential nature of the profit-making process. Consider then Figure 5, in which the history of the firm

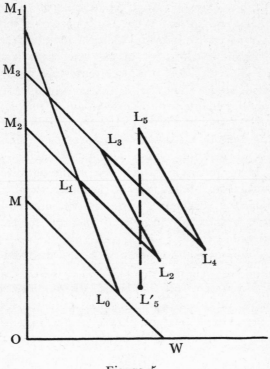

Figure 5.

is sketched for a few successive operations. We start with the firm at the point L_0, with the price equal to the slope of MW . Now suppose the next day the price rises: the opportunity line steepens to L_0L_1, and the firm sells wheat at this higher price, moving to L_1. The next day the price drops, the opportunity line flattens to L_1L_2, and the firm moves to L_2. So it proceeds to positions L_3, L_4, L_5 and so on. What is happening is that, as a result of successive manipulations of the asset structure, the position of the firm in the asset field is moving further out. L_5, for instance, represents more wheat and more money than the intitial position L_0. It would be equally possible for the firm to move from L_5 to L_0, by buying dear and selling cheap—indeed this is frequently done by unsuccessful business men! This is the process of making losses. The profit-making process, then, is a process in which the manipulations of an asset structure through various forms of transformation —production, exchange, consumption, but not distribution*—results in an overall increase in the total quantity of assets.

Now, however, the inherent difficulty involved in the

---

*The problem of dividends, distributions out of profits, or of entrepreneurial withdrawals from the accounts of a business should be mentioned briefly here. A "withdrawal" from a business account differs from an asset transformation in that it represents the diminution in one asset (usually money) without any corresponding increase in any other asset. It is measure of profits becomes clear. The profit-making process is one in which a complex aggregate of many different kinds of assets is in some way increased. If this increase is to be measured the heterogeneous mass of physical assets must be reduced to a homogeneous financial statement. To do this, however, each item must be multiplied by a valuation coefficient to reduce its "value" to the *numeraire* (dollars). Then the question arises *what* valuation coefficient should be used? The value of the net worth (and hence those changes in the value of net worth which are the measure of profit) depends in large measure on the system of valuation. And the odd fact is that almost any system of valuation will yield some anomalous results.

---

a process therefore which differs fundamentally from the processes of asset transformation by which the diminution in one asset always results in the increase of another. The profit "making" process is that by which the net worth of an organization is increased through successive asset transformations and revaluations. The profit-distribution process is that by which the net worth is decreased through the withdrawal of assets (usually of money). Thus in Figure 5 suppose that at the point L_5 the entrepreneur withdrew a sum of money $L_5 L'_5$ from the business: in the case of a corporation this might represent a cash dividend. The position of the enterprise moves from L_5 to L'_5—from which point the profit-making process may start all over again.

51

Consider, for instance, the effects of valuation of inventory at market price. In Figure 5 this would mean that on Day 1 net worth would suddenly rise to OM_1; on Day 2 it would fall to OM_2, even though the move from L_1 and L_2 in response to the lower price is "profitable" in the sense that it lays the groundwork for further advances when the price rises once more. Thus, on this principle, the firm seems to suffer an alteration of profit and loss, profit when price rises, loss when it falls, even though it is precisely these alterations of high and low price which enable the firm to make profits at all! In the short run, at any rate, there is a curious element of inconsistency here even though in the long run the measure may work itself out.

The results of the various methods of inventory accounting (last-in-first-out, first-in-first-out, or constant price variations) can be analyzed by this method. No matter what the method of accounting, there is a certain arbitrariness always implied in the measure of profits because the profit-making process is not a simple linear growth. It is a process whereby the asset structure grows in many dimensions, in some dimensions faster than others and in some dimensions perhaps the quantity of the assets may even be declining. Accounting is the attempt to reduce this multi-dimensional phenomenon to a simple linear scale of dollars. Because the basic phenomenon is multi-dimensional, the attempt to reduce this growth of asset-structures (the essence of the profit-making process) to a simple linear scale, is bound to involve arbitrary assumptions and a certain violation of reality. We run into exactly the same problem in the construction of index numbers, where it is well-known that there is not a single "true" index number of prices or outputs. This is because the reality is multi-dimensional and any attempt to express a multi-dimensional set as a simple number must involve arbitrary assumptions. It is less well recognized that even the simplest accounting procedures really involve the same problem, perhaps because of the deceptive homogeneity of the dollar-values in financial statements. The arbitrary nature of the procedures involved in either accounting or in the construction of index numbers is no argument against the practice of these procedures. They are necessary because the human mind cannot easily handle many dimensions at the same time. The mind constantly seeks to reduce heterogeneous aggregates to some single homogeneous dimension. Statistical and accounting procedures, while they violate in some degree the nature of the multi-dimensional universe with which they deal, also increase our knowledge of it by a process of rough summarization.

Thus, suppose we were given two long price lists containing a thousand items. We are then asked the difference between the two lists. The mind cannot easily visualize the difference between the two points in a space of a thousand dimensions! If, however, we make a price index and are informed that the index corresponding to the first list is 100 and to the second list is 134, we feel that our knowledge, or at least our perception of an important aspect of the two lists, is increased. This is possible even though the index can only be constructed by making certain arbitrary asumptions about the "weights" of the prices summarized and even though equally plausible assumptions may give us quite widely differing answers.

Similarly, in the case of accounting procedures, if we are faced with two physical balance sheets containing a thousand items—so many tons of this, pounds of that, dollars of debt, and so on—we cannot easily perceive the direct relationship between them. The accountant therefore makes a financial statement, much as the statistician makes an index number, by valuing all the heterogeneous items in terms of a common denominator. If we are then told that one balance sheet represents a net total of $1,000,000 and the other a net total of $1,200,000, again we feel that we know more about them than before. This is in spite of the fact that the two numbers cannot possibly be *substitutes* for the thousand-dimensional complexity of the balance sheets themselves and are necessarily derived from procedures which are arbitrary in the sense that other procedures, giving somewhat different answers, make just about as much sense.

So far we have considered profit merely as an absolute amount and not as a rate of return. A rate of return is a rate of growth and the rate of profit therefore is the rate of growth of net worth. The same difficulties that we encounter in measuring absolute amounts of profit also occur when we are trying to measure a rate of return. On most accounting measures the growth of the net worth through time will be a highly irregular one, alternating rapid leaps in advance with slower movements or even with retreats. If we reckon the rate of growth of net worth simply as a percentage of the net worth at the beginning of each period, the rate of return likewise will exhibit irregular movements which may have nothing to do with the underlying conditions of the enterprise. Between any two points in the history of the enterprise we can calculate an average rate of return—i.e., that rate of growth of the initial value of the net worth which would produce the final value of the net worth, after allowance has been made for withdrawals. We think of the initial value growing at a certain rate, being reduced once in a while by withdrawals, but continuing immediately to grow steadily and finally reaching the level where it actually stands at the end of the period. The actual course of the net worth will be very different from the steady growth course, but the average rate of growth is a summary of its general trend.

The situation is complicated further when there is a debt, for debt also grows at a rate equal to its rate of interest. We have then a kind of race between the assets side and the liabilities side of the balance sheet. The rate of growth of the *net* worth is then dependent on the extent to which the assets can grow faster than the liabilities—that is, on the extent by which the rate of return of the total of assets (the "average efficiency of capital") exceeds the rate of interest on the debt. The situation becomes still more complicated when we try to put the problem in marginal terms, comparing marginal efficiencies of capital with marginal rates of interest on increments to assets and to debt respectively.

We can now see some of the difficulties which are inherent in the apparently simple notion of profit maximization. The main difficulty is that the quantity which is supposed to be maximized does not really exist! It would be unkind to call it a figment of the accountant's imagination but it is certainly a product of the accountant's rituals. The difficulty of measurement is seen clearly in Figure 5: the profit-making *process* is the generally outward movement in the field through successive asset-transformations, $L_0L_1L_2L_3$, etc. The measure of profit on the vertical scale $MM_1M_2M_3$, etc., depends on the technique of valuations employed. The figure however reveals a yet more fundamental difficulty in the notion of profit maximization. If we knew in advance exactly what the various prices on the various days were going to be, it is evident that the wider the swings (the more wheat is bought on the days of low prices and the more is sold on the days of high prices) the more rapidly on the whole will the firm increase assets—that is, move outward and upward in the field of the diagram.

The maximization of profits, under conditions of

certainty in expectations, then becomes a problem in boundary maxima. It is not susceptible to the marginal analysis at all. The rule is simply to move as far as possible in the direction of holding *commodity* when the price is going to rise, and to move as far as possible in the direction of holding *money* when the price is going to fall. If there are perfect capital markets—that is, if it is possible to borrow any amount of money or commodity on terms which do not depend on the amount borrowed—there are no limits at all to the rate of profit. The firm would then borrow an infinite amount of money and hold an infinite amount of commodity whenever the price was going to rise. Likewise it would borrow an infinite amount of commodity and hold an infinite amount of money whenever the price was going to fall, the rate of profit being also infinite! The absurdity of this conclusion points up the fact that one of two things must limit the rate of profit. *Either* there must be some sort of imperfection in markets or in other transformation functions—i.e., the rate of transformation of one asset into another in some sense must "worsen" through price or interest changes as the first asset continued to be transformed into the second. *Or* there must be uncertainty as to the future, making the possibilities of loss as well as the possibilities of gain greater as assets are transformed one into another. Thus suppose in Figure 5 we proceed upwards from L_o in the direction of M_1, selling wheat and acquiring money in the expectation of a fall in the price of wheat and a subsequent movement along a path such as L_1L_2. If we are certain that the price of wheat is going to fall then the further we move in the direction of L_oM_1 the better. Suppose, however, that we have an uneasy feeling that there *might* be a rise in the price rather than a fall. Then the further we move along L_oM_1 the more we stand to lose if in fact there is a rise in price, though equally, the more we stand to gain if there is a fall. If now, as we move along the transformation function, the fear of loss rises faster than the hope of gain, at some point the marginal advantage from the hope of gain is just balanced by the marginal disadvantage of the fear of loss. It will not be advantageous to proceed beyond this point because of the uncertanties involved.

We now seem to be back at something much more like the marginal analysis, not maximizing a profit in any accounting sense—this being impossible in the presence of uncertainty—but maximizing utility or advantage in a broad sense.

We run into much the same problem, even under conditions of certainty, if the markets for the various assets are imperfect. It is then not impossible to transform one asset into another in indefinite quantities without loss. Under these circumstances it may well be reasonable to prefer a combination of assets with a lower accounting value to a combination with a higher value. This would be true if the former represents a more desirable *structure* of assets—better proportioned, less open to sudden and unexpected, unfavorable changes, more

58

liquid, etc. The simple profit maximization theory assumes, in effect, that it is only the total value of assets which is significant to the firm, not the form or composition of these assets.

This is to say that the theory of profit maximization is only applicable to the case in which all markets are perfect, where there is no difficulty in transforming any asset into any other, and where the *form* of the asset structure is unimportant. Also, it is applicable only where there is no uncertainty so that we never have to balance lucrativity against security. If, however, under these idyllic circumstances, the maximum profit is to be finite there must be diminishing returns in some sense. In fact, this is precisely the case for which the theory of profit maximization was originally conceived. Economists have not generally realized the damage done to the fundamental principle of profit maximization by the attempt to extend the analysis to imperfect markets and uncertain futures.

If we now reduce the marginal analysis to the maximizing of utility, are we saying anything at all? Utility is such a vague, unmeasurable concept that the reader may be pardoned if he doubts whether the concept is of use for any purpose other than passing examinations. To raise this question, however, is to penetrate the very heart of the marginal analysis. It is to understand not only the strength of the criticisms made against it but also why it persists in spite of these criticisms. Usually the marginal analysis is criticized as an analysis of behavior. However, the marginal analysis, in its generalized form, is *not* an analysis of *behavior* but an analysis of *advantage*. It is not a psychology or an analysis of actual behavior. It is more akin to an *ethic* or an analysis of normative positions. It only becomes an analysis of behavior if we make the further assumption that people always act according to their best advantage. In the case of individuals this assumption is only occasionally true.

People are motivated, even in economic activity, by traditional behavior, by the habit of following well-established rules of thumb, and by response patterns which are derived from sources in the subconscious and have little or nothing to do with the careful weighing of advantage against disadvantage. The passions constantly war with the intellect and even St. Paul complained that, "The good that I would, I do not; but the evil which I would not, that I do." (Rom. 7:19). Nevertheless it is important to have an analysis of advantage even if this is not an analysis of behavior. It is important for two reasons. It is important in itself because it is useful to have some kind of standard by which actual behavior may be judged. If it makes some sense to castigate certain types of behavior as stupid then we must have some notion of the sensible. It then makes sense to clarify the sensible. The analysis of advantage is also important because, in the mass, there must be some tendency for actual behavior to move towards the most advantageous behavior if only because advantageous behavior is likely to have survival value. Those who do not behave in the most advantageous manner do not ultimately survive. If this is the case then the assumption that individuals actually behave to their best advantage is more likely to be true in the aggregate than it is in the individual case. That is to say, aggregative propositions, based on the assumption that individuals maximize advantage, may be quite good descriptions of the behavior of the aggregates. This has been, after all, the economist's primary interest. Even if the original assumption is not a good description of the behavior of any single individual the individual deviations tend to cancel out in the aggregate. This point has been made eloquently by Dr. A. A. Alchian.

We must not, however, be carried away by an enthusiasm for aggregates. The concept of maximum advantage and the concept of maximum survival value are not the same. They may be equated but they should not be identified. And there is no more necessity in the assumption that behavior drifts toward the position of maximum survival value for organization than there is in the assumption that behavior drifts toward the position of maximum advantage. There are, for instance, *heroic* ethical systems in which advantage is not couched in terms of survival at all (except perhaps in a very long-run sense) and certainly not in terms of individual survival. Individuals who differ as widely as the saint and the soldier may hold ethical systems (as expressed in our terms in advantage or utility functions) which

61

attach high values to sacrifice, to service, and to self-giving, which are certainly not conducive to individual survival. One recalls, for instance, the almost unbelievable story of Canudos and the followers of Antonio the Counselor who, in the otherwise prosaic 1890's, fought off the Brazilian army literally to the last man. Nevertheless, in the more prosaic world of ordinary economic life, there is at least nothing absurd in the assumption that behavior according to maximum advantage is likely to have survival value and that the firm that succeeds in maximizing its profits (other advantage factors being held constant) is likely to do better than a firm which fails to do so.

From the point of view of behavior theory the great weakness of the marginal analysis, even in its generalized form, is the absence of any information system. It is important to realize, however, that if we cannot *know* where the optimum, or the point of maximum advantage, is located, we obviously cannot move toward it.

Thus the marginal analysis does not describe a true *equilibrium* system. In general the information system of a firm or of any economic organization does not record, except in an extremely vague and broad sense, the divergences between the actual position of the organization and the optimum. As we shall see more clearly in the next chapter some information system of this kind is absolutely essential to any theory of behavior. There can be a marked divergence between the actual position of an organization and its optimum position, measured on any standard, and the organization might be quite unaware of the fact. This is likely to be true in periods of rapid change when the old rules of thumb and traditional modes of behavior (which may have been well adapted to give a position close to the optimum in more stable times) mislead firms into adopting policies very far from the optimum. Thus, when much against their will, the American railroads in the 1930's were forced to reduce their passenger fares, they found to their great surprise that the increase in passenger traffic was so great that their financial returns were improved. Here was a clear case of the inertia of large organizations operating largely by traditional rules which led to a gross failure to reach optimum positions.

It is interesting to observe that there has been an important movement, within the last ten years or less, to improve the information system of organizations in directions which are indicated by the marginal analysis. The movement, which is known as "Operations Research," originated in the armed forces during the second World War but has spread rapidly to the business world. It involves an elaborate set of techniques involving mathematics much more advanced than the simple differential calculus which is used in the marginal analysis. Nevertheless the basic principle of the "optimum"— that is of finding the "best" position of a set of opportunities—lies at the heart of it. It can be applied to the routing of ships, to the hunting of submarines, to finding product mix from an oil refinery, or to inventory control. It is curious that at the very time when some economists were boldly engaged in trying to throw the maximization principle out the front door the engineers were sneaking it in the back door in the form of "linear programming" and Operations Research.

We may once more test the skill of the economist (myself for instance) who is skilled in the techniques of the marginal analysis by supposing that he advises the president of a large corporation. What sort of advice, if any, will his skills enable him to give? In this case the quality of the advice may depend more on an awareness of the concrete reality around him than on his peculiar skill in the marginal analysis. Indeed, if I were the president of a corporation, I would take some care to avoid hiring an economist adviser whose *sole* skill was the marginal analysis! Nevertheless, if the adviser is sensible he knows that a knowledge of the marginal analysis will certainly do him no harm and will give him means for organizing his thoughts; means which are not available to the untrained person.

The marginal analysis will direct his attention towards the *problem* of the optimum even if it gives him no simple rule for finding it. It is useful to be able to "think marginally"—to think in terms of the little bit more and the little bit less, the careful weighing of gains and losses from small changes. The marginal analysis will also direct attention to certain things which are not normally in the information system of a firm such as the nature of the firm's demand and supply curves. At least it may lead to the questioning of the tacit and almost subconscious hypotheses which every business man makes about these subterranean relationships. The marginal analysis will make him suspicious of averages and behavior based on averages—averages being a form of information which is relatively easy to get but which may be highly misleading once obtained.

A familiarity with the marginal analysis may lead to a turn of mind which sees clearly the difference between transformation or opportunity relationships on the one hand and preference functions on the other. Our adviser should always be on the lookout for unexpected relationships among the many variables with which a firm has to deal for the reason that solutions to problems in one place may create three worse problems elsewhere. His should be the warning voice reminding management that the enterprise is a whole and must be looked at as a whole and that the various policies of different departments or different aspects of the enterprise must be coordinated.

Finally, because he has in his head a greatly simplified model of what an enterprise looks like, he may be more sensitive to those changes in environment which make old rules obsolete. These are the changes which force an enterprise, if it is to survive, to make constant adaptations in its products, in its prices, and in its overall policies, to the changing scene around it. Not all these virtues of course can be ascribed solely to a knowledge of the marginal analysis. But skill in the marginal analysis, as a vital instrument rather than as a textbook trick, will contribute to all of them. Perhaps the economist should be hired after all!

Organization and Communication

CHAPTER III

Can Economics find a savior
In general theories of behavior?
In feedbacks, servos, Homeostasis
And similar unlikely places?

THE MARGINAL ANALYSIS is not what is has sometimes been thought to be—a theory of economic behavior. By admitting this we have rescued the marginal analysis as a normative theory of maximum advantage but we are still left with what looks like a substantial hole in the structure of economic theory. For, as we have seen, the economist cannot afford to be totally indifferent to the behavior of men and of organizations even if his prime interest is in the behavior of commodities. He is in a less favored position than the astronomer who can conveniently neglect the hypothesis that the planets are moved by angels because whether they are so moved or not, angels behave with such beautiful regularity that their behavior presents no problems and hence can be neglected. As long as the angels obey the law of gravity their presence or absence is of no concern to the astronomer.

The planets of the economist—his vast universe of prices, quantities of commodities, and other assets—are not moved by angels but by men. And the behavior of men, unfortunately, is neither as simple nor as reliable as that of angels—a fact which forces the economist, almost against his will, to take an interest in human behavior. It also forces economics, even without pressure from the Ford Foundation, to be in part a *behavioral science*. Let us then take some simple theories of behavior and see how they might possibly be incorporated into economics by applying them to the behavior of economic organizations.

The term *behavior* is something which can properly be applied only to organizations or organisms. We may perhaps stretch the word by talking about the behavior of a planet or of a stone thrown into the air but on the whole the problems of what we usually think of as behavior apply to such things as the cell, the bacterium, the animal, the man, the family, the firm, the nation, and the church, all of which are characterized by organization. The theory of behavior, therefore, should properly include also a theory of organization since the subject of the verb "to behave" is generally an organization of some sort, whether a relatively complex organization like the cell, or a relatively simple organization like the Federal Reserve System. We should not perhaps be fussy about the exact definition of an organization since there is no very sharp line in the universe at which organizations begin. Nevertheless all organizations, from the smallest living cell to the largest social organization, have certain things in common. It is not absurd therefore to build models of organizations—that is, simplified intellectual constructs, or ideal types, which will have general applicability.

All organizations can be characterized by something like a physical balance sheet or position statement—i.e., a list, or maybe a map of their identifiable parts, whether these parts are the mitochondria and other subcellular structures within the cell, the assets and liabilities of a corporation, or the institutions and characteristics of a state.

In general these parts are subject to three kinds of transformations. First, there may be simple consumption or loss, in which the part is lost to the outside environment or disintegrates into parts which are not functioning members of the organization. Second, there may be internal transformations (production) in which certain parts are recombined into other parts—as, for instance, chemical transformations within the cell, or production transformations within the corporation, or institutional reorganizations within a state. Then finally, there may be exchanges with the environment—metabolic exchange in the cell in which certain elements or compounds are

69

taken in from the outside and certain others released to the outside, or exchange in the firm in which commodities are released to the outside and money is taken in, or vice versa.

All organizations, no matter how humble, are also characterized by a learning or an adaptive process by which the activity of the organization becomes modified in response to repeated experiences of an unfavorable or favorable nature. All organizations also exhibit a capacity for growth and development which seems to come from some mysterious inner source. Every organization has but a limited number of potential lines of development: the acorn never grows into an elm, though it may of course be prevented from growing into an oak. Similarly, the young railroad does not grow up to be a chain store firm, nor does the young state develop into a church. The fact that a Linen Company in Scotland became a bank, or that a young man on occasion apparently turns into a young woman, merely provides the exceptions that prove the rule.

Probably the simplest theory of behavior of organizations is the theory of homeostasis—or perhaps one should say that the simplest *form* of behavior is homeostatic behavior. Homeostasis is the ability of an organization to maintain a given structure in the face of a changing environment. One of the simplest examples of a homeostatic apparatus is the familiar thermostat, designed to maintain constancy of temperature in the neighborhood of the recording instrument. The homeostatic value

70

in this case is the temperature for which the thermostat is set. If the actual temperature, as recorded by the thermometer, exceeds the homeostatic value, behavior within the system takes place in order to correct this situation—the furnace is turned off. If the actual temperature is less than the homeostatic value behavior again takes place to correct the situation—the furnace is turned on. Large numbers of mechanisms of this sort exist in the living organism maintaining constancy of its physical and chemical states—temperatures, pressures, and blood composition.

The theory of homeostasis also applies to economic organizations. In fact, about the simplest possible theory of behavior of economic organizations is the theory of homeostasis of the physical balance sheet or *position statement.* We suppose that there are certain quantities of various kinds of assets and liabilities—i.e., a physical balance sheet. The firm wants to maintain these quantities, that is, if any item in this balance sheet is disturbed or changed, action or behavior of some kind will take place to correct the disturbance and bring the balance sheet back to where it was before, just as the thermostat sets the furnace in motion if the temperature is too low. The simplest changes are those which are involved in buying and selling. Thus, suppose a firm sells 100 bushels of wheat for $200. This transaction increases its money stock by $200 and decreases its wheat stock by 100 bushels, thus disturbing the previous balance sheet. In order to restore the previous position the firm must now, in some way, acquire 100 bushels of wheat and get rid of money to the value of $200. This it may do by buying wheat again or producing wheat by purchasing factors of production and transforming them into wheat.

Why, on this theory, would anybody ever do anything —why not simply preserve the sacred position by permitting nothing to leave or enter the holy vessel of the enterprise in a Nirvana of perpetual stability and inaction? The answer is; even on the assumption of simple homeostasis of the balance sheet, things happen to assets which are not under the direct control of the firm and therefore compel the firm to adopt a course of countervailing action. There is, for instance, decay and depreciation, the corruption of moth and rust. An economic organization which simply sits down with a pile of assets will find, after a few years, that the assets have crumbled into decay. The miser is about the only example of the homeostasis of inaction and even the miser is likely to find in these days that inflation has eaten away the value of his hoard just as surely as moths eat his clothes or rats nibble his grain. Furthermore, in so far as the economic organization includes living organisms among its assets, it will find the iron law of consumption applies to them with peculiar force. Breakfast, alas, depreciates almost entirely by lunchtime and in order to maintain the living organism a constant stream of destruction must be suffered, food going down its insatiable maw, clothing wearing out on its abrasive back, and entertainment constantly being engulfed by its unbounded lust for pleasure. Even worse, if the economic organization happens to be a firm, customers persist in buying things from it: it sits in a market place in which it is forced to cry its wares and the cry is answered by outsiders who persistently upset its nice equilibrium by thrusting money upon it in exchange for goods, money which it is then forced to spend in the replacement of the goods torn from its shelves.

Because of the depreciation of its fixed capital, an economic organization is forced to make gross profits even if it does not make net profits. This must be done simply to maintain its position. When a customer buys goods from it the firm cannot go out and buy them back from the same or another customer. It must somehow manage to replace the goods sold by the sacrifice of *less* money than it received for them in order that it may have resources with which to repair the ravages of depreciation and decay. Out of the $200 received for the 100 bushels of wheat, the firm must somehow manage to set aside a certain amount, say $50, for the maintenance of its fixed assets (including the bodies and personalities of its owners and its employees) and must somehow manage to replace the 100 bushels of wheat by spending only $150. It is this dismal necessity which forces economic organizations into production and prevents us from having a pure exchange economy in which goods perpetually circulate from hand to hand in an endless game of hunt-the-slipper.

We come close to the pure exchange economy in the

securities market where the assets that circulate (being disembodied spirits) are somewhat more durable than the physical assets they represent. But even here the rule of moth and rust takes over and the securities of once prosperous firms crumble in the dust. In the market for physical commodities, however, consumption dominates the scene and so forces production upon the economy if the physical balance sheet is to be maintained.

One of the interesting things about the theory of homeostasis of the physical balance sheet is the ease with which it lends itself to aggregation and to those difficult jumps from theories of individual behavior to theories of aggregate behavior. It is clear that in a society in which the maintenance of physical balance sheets was the universal rule all consumption would lead, immediately and directly, to production. Suppose for instance that I look in my drawer one day and find the normal agencies of wear and washing machines have reduced my stock of socks below what I consider necessary. In order to restore this disproportion in my asset structure I go out and buy half a dozen pairs of socks. The store then finds itself with too few socks and too much money and buys socks from the wholesaler, who likewise finds himself with too few socks and too much money so he buys from the manufacturer, who also finds himself short of socks and flush with money so he buys yarn and labor and makes more socks. This depletes the stocks of the yarn merchant who in turn orders yarn from the spinner who in turn gets more wool from the sheep. In such an economy there would be no accumulation—production and consumption would be equal and, if consumption is a function of total production, the equilibrium output will be given at the point on the consumption function where production is just sufficient to call forth an equal amount of consumption. This is the classical *stationary state*.

We know that neither society nor the individual organization is stationary. In very few organizations do we have simple homeostasis in the sense of maintaining a condition as described above. The question arises, therefore, whether the concept of homeostasis is applicable to growing organizations and societies. The answer is a qualified yes. There is certainly no reason why rates of growth should not in themselves be homeostatic variables. In the case of the firm there may be some ideal or homeostatic rate of overall growth measured by net worth, by asset totals, by annual income, by turnover, or by sales—whatever variable strikes the entrepreneur as most significant. If growth is slower than this ideal rate forces are brought into play to speed it up—more capital is ploughed back into the business, less is distributed in dividends, or more efforts are put into increasing overall profits. Similarly, if growth is faster than the ideal rate, efforts may be slackened, more earnings are distributed, and less kept in the business. I understand, for instance, that in the DuPont Company the ideal rate is held to be about 6% per annum; that overall growth rates lower than this are held to be matters of concern; that growth rates higher than this may lead to some slackening in the pace of activity or in the pinch of parsimony.

It is not unreasonable to regard the profit rate as a homeostatic variable and to assume that, instead of seeking to maximize profits, the firm generally seeks to maintain what it regards as a reasonable rate. If actual profits fall below the homeostatic rate management becomes agitated, holds conferences, schemes schemes, and devises devices to cut costs or to increase revenues and so raise profits again. If it rises above the reasonable rate managerial activity slackens off, more golf is played, labor and customers are given concessions more easily and less pressure is placed on engineers to cut costs. The principle of a homeostatic rate of profit does not contradict the broad interpretation of the marginal analysis given in the previous chapter since we merely suppose that "advantage" is at a maximum when the level of profits is "right," and that profits either above or below this level make management feel uneasy. Apart from some assumption such as this it is very difficult to interpret the behavior of many large American corporations which frequently allow opportunities for making abnormally high profits escape them because they do not want to be accused of gouging or profiteering. The restrained price policy of the automobile companies after World War II and the DuPont Company in the period of acute nylon shortage are interesting cases in point. It may also be observed that small businesses and individual entrepreneurs often do not feel this compunction. The noble price policies of the automobile companies went to swell the ignoble profits of the dealers rather than to create good will by swelling the pockets of the public, as any economist should have been able to predict.

Thus it is rewarding to look for homeostatic variables as an explanation of the actual behavior of firms. Some firms, for instance, have a morbid fear of debt. They are not happy as long as there are any contractual liabilities in their balance sheets. Other firms have no such inhibitions yet it is not unreasonable to postulate certain homeostatic values for debt in the case of each firm. That is, for each firm there will be some volume or proportion of debt which they feel is "too much", some other volume or proportion which they feel is "too little". Similarly some firms are jealous of their good labor relationships and are prepared to pay to keep them that way; other firms may be indifferent to the quality of their labor relations or may even prefer to live in a continual commotion with high labor turnover and constant industrial strife. The same may be said of some firms attitude toward public relations. For some the homeostatic value of public relations is very high and they seek to cultivate good will by everything from honest service to cajolery while others follow the maxim, "The public be damned."

Useful as the homeostasis concept is, especially as a

guide to empirical research, it does not apply to all problems of behavior. To return for instance to the problem of growth. It may be true that for certain periods in their lives both firms and individuals may set a homeostatic value for the rate of growth of their businesses or their private capital. This, however, is not enough. Growth cannot be kept up at a constant rate for ever—otherwise there would soon be only one organization in the whole universe! The growth pattern of *every* organization exhibits a characteristic form. The rate of growth tends to be slow at first, rises to a maximum, and declines again as the organization ages. The problem of the life cycle or the growth curve cannot be answered by any appeal to the relatively simple theory of homeostasis. The homeostasis theory applies fairly well to stationary states and even dynamic situations in which the movement or the rate of growth is stationary. It cannot apply to those mysterious "tides in the affairs of men"—and of all organisms and organizations— which carry them to maturity and to eventual decay.

Some explanation of the forces leading to declining rates of growth can be found in the principle of diminishing returns to scale. An organization cannot grow without becoming larger and as it becomes larger its various parts change proportionately. This is true of all organizations, both biological and social. It may be called the *principle of non-proportional change*. It is based on the proposition that a uniform change in the linear dimensions of any structure increases the areas

78

as the square and the volumes as the cube of the linear increase. Thus, doubling the linear dimensions quadruples the areas and octuples the volumes of any structure. Therefore growth in size changes the proportions of many significant quantities since some aspects of an organization depend on lengths, some on areas, and some on volumes. This is why insects, which breathe through the skin, cannot be much longer than about three inches. The larger a body the greater the volumes to be supported in proportion to the supporting surfaces. In order to overcome these changes in proportions organizations develop specialized devices such as complex nervous systems to overcome the linearity of communication or complex convolutions in the lungs, the bowels, and the brain in order to overcome the superficial nature of breathing, digesting and thinking. There is a limit, however, to the devices that can be evolved—a limit of size represented apparently, in the case of living organisms, by the blue whale.

The same process of modifying the organism to compensate for increased size can also be observed in social organizations. Large organizations must develop complicated communication systems, elaborate executive procedures, and highly formalized structures compared to the informality of small-scale organizations. This must be done to overcome the increasing inadequacy of communication systems which are essentially linear in structure as compared to the interactions of the organization which are multi-dimensional in structure. The size of organizations is ultimately limited *internally* by the inability to devise further compensations for the inadequate proportions of the communications system. This could be called the *brontosaurus principle* after its most distinguished exponent in natural history. If, however, size is ultimately limited, then growth must eventually slow down.

There is another reason for the limitation of size and the slowing down of growth. As an organization expands the environment into which it expands becomes increasingly unfavorable. Thus, a new sect or a new party finds it easy to attract adherents at first. Once all the easily-won members have been gathered into the fold the task of expansion becomes much harder. In the case of a firm this principle expresses itself as an imperfection in its buying or selling markets. Once it has attracted all the easy customers it must either lower its price or increase its selling cost in order to expand sales. This is a deterioration of its *terms of trade* with the environment. This imperfection may be of particular importance in the market for loans where a firm may find that after a certain point it has to pay exorbitant rates of interest or it may not even be able to get loans on any terms.

We do know something about the forces that bring growth to an end. What we do not understand are the forces that initiate it. What is it within the seed or the egg that cannot be contained and explodes into a tree or a man? What makes a small state grow into a great empire or a small business grow into a great enterprise when other states and other businesses seem content to remain in happy obscurity? What is it that forces one culture up the rough but exciting road of economic development while another culture slumbers for centuries in stationary equilibrium? These are the greatest unanswered questions of the biological and the social sciences. Indeed, it may be that in these days of the expanding universe the development of the whole universe is part of the incomprehensible mystery of the seed.

There are other avenues for pursuing the theory of growth. However, I wish to return to the more humble ground of homeostasis and inquire in more detail into the nature of the homeostatic process and how an organization or organism manages to keep its constants constant! We have hinted at the machinery but it is useful to examine it in more detail, especially from the point of view of economic behavior.

Homeostasis always involves what we now designate as a *feedback,* or a servo-mechanism. This consists essentially of six parts or *organs.* First there must be a *receptor* which is capable of detecting divergences between the actual value of the significant variable and the ideal or homeostatic value. This is the thermometer of the thermostat, the sense organs of the animal, the information-gatherers of the firm. The receptor lines of communication or *data-communicators,* capable of transmitting the information picked up by the receptors, must

81

lead to a third organ, the *executive* or interpreter. Thus in the thermostat there are wires which carry messages from the thermometer to the control. In the body there are nerves and blood streams which carry messages from the sense organs to the nerve centers and the brain. In the firm, or other social organization, there are lines of communication which carry messages to management, or the executive. The business of the executive is to transform the data-information he receives into instructions-information or orders. These, in turn, go out from him along the fourth organ, the *orders-communicator*. The orders-communicators are the wires from the control to the furnace, the nerves from the brain and other nerve centers to the muscles, the lines of communication from the executive to the labor force. The orders-communicator leads to the fifth organ, the *effector,* which is capable of receiving orders and transforming these into effects of some kind, which are finally transmitted by *effect-transmitters* to the initial environment. The furnace, the muscles, the plant or the factory are the effectors; the pipes and radiators, the organs of movement, and the means of transportation are the effect-transmitters. Figure 6 shows the whole apparatus in diagrammatic form.

These six organs are the bare minimum for the functioning of a homeostatic system. The system will function only if the movements are in the right direction. Thus, if the receptor indicates that the variable in the environment is *below* the homeostatic value, the communication of this information to the executive must result in orders to the effector which, when carried out, will have the effect of *raising* the variable in the environment. If the variable is *above* the homeostatic value the operations of the systems must lower it.

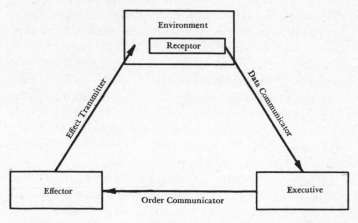

Figure 6.

It should be observed that the immediate effect of a once-round operation of the system does not have to be exactly proportionate to the gap between the ideal and the recorded values of the homeostatic variable. The system will operate as long as the effect is *roughly proportionate* to the size of the gap and as long as the effect is in the right direction of closing the gap. This is the feed-back: the effect of the decisions of the executive are

83

fed back to him through the data communicators and as long as a gap exists there will be a tendency to operate so as to close it. Once the gap is closed the operations cease, though this does not mean that the system as such is disbanded. This is a proposition of the utmost importance to economics because it means that the *control* of a system does not depend on exact prediction of its fluctuations but only on the ability to predict the direction of change and its order of magnitude. The business cycle may be interpreted as a homeostatic system of too little sensitivity. The control of the business cycle simply involves the ability to increase the sensitivity of the system without perverting its direction. We do not, therefor, involve ourselves in the impossible task of predicting what would have happened in the next twelve months if somebody hadn't taken steps to stop it!

As long as there are any time lags between the various stages of the system, as in practice there must be, systems of this kind are almost certain to set up cycles. Thus, suppose we start with a position where the recorded value is below the ideal value. This information results in action which raises the variable, an action which will be initiated as long as the divergence exists. Suppose now that the operations of the effector reduce the gap to zero. When this information is communicated to the executive it (or he) will order the effector to cease the operation which is increasing the variable. However, these orders take time and in the meantime the effector is still increasing the variable, sending it *above* the ideal value.

This information will cause the executive to order a reversal of the effector's operation which may eventually bring the variable somewhat below the ideal level again and so the cycle continues. In some cases, depending mainly on the sensitivity of the system and the nature of the time lags, the oscillations of the system may be noticeable and permanent. The perpetual oscillation of the house temperature in a house heated by a hand-fired, and especially by a professor-fired, furnace between the two extremes of too hot and too cold is a nice case in point. In extreme cases the oscillations may be explosive, in which case the system will simply break up. In most cases the oscillations tend to be damped so that in the absence of any new disturbances the system will settle down at the ideal value of the variable.

In any complex organization, such as a living organism or a social organization, a great many of these servo-mechanisms are likely to be functioning at different levels. Thus, in the human body there are innumerable such mechanisms which operate below the level of consciousness, maintaining the stability of the chemical and physical constitution of the body. There are also mechanisms which operate at a more conscious level, in which for instance hunger leads us to eat, thirst leads us to drink, a desire for love and companionship leads us to marriage, and an awareness of ignorance leads us to study. In the business enterprise we also find a great many such mechanisms at all levels, some even built into the machines themselves. Foremen detect small divergen-

85

ces between their ideal and the reality of the operation of their particular section and take measures to close these small gaps without even bothering their superiors.

At all levels of the hierarchy the main task of management is constantly to receive information, to compare this information with some ideal, and to issue orders which, they believe, will set in motion operations to close the homeostatic gaps. It is clear that management, in the sense of performing some of the functions of an executive in a servo-mechanism, is found at all levels of an organization and at all levels of society. The assembly-line worker senses a gap between his position and his capabilities and so looks around for another job or attends night school. The chairman of the corporation is concerned with the gap between what he feels the structure of the whole organization should be and what his source of information pictures it in actuality. As we rise in the scale of management we become less concerned with the functioning of a given organization and more concerned with the nature of the organization itself but we never get away from the basic executive function of receiving information and translating it into instructions.

The above model throws a good deal of light on the nature of organization, especially the large-scale organization. One may say almost paradoxically that the main purpose of organizational structure is to *prevent* information reaching the higher executives. Each executive can handle only so much information—if he gets too much, or the wrong kind, he suffers a breakdown and fails to digest, analyze, interpret and transmute it into the appropriate instructions. If we think of the executive—at any level—as a kind of specialized information-grinder, receiving one kind of information on the one hand and sending out another kind of information on the other hand, it is clear that any given executive will have a certain capacity, just as any production apparatus for transforming inputs into outputs has a capacity. Barnard makes the point that the higher we go on the executive scale the main function is more apt to be the veto function—that is, to select among the various positive ideas and suggestions which come up the line rather than the creative function of suggesting new ideas.

> In every modern corporation
> Are channels of communication
> Along which lines, from foot to crown,
> Ideas flow up, and vetoes down.

This line of argument leads to several promising avenues of research into the behavior of economic organizations—and indeed of any type of organization. The first is the idea of information itself. This is basic to the whole theory of organization and behavior. Information is the essential difference between purely mechanical systems of constant physical response to constant physical stimuli and "organizational" or "living" systems with varying response to constant physical stimuli, depending on the "significance" of the stimuli in an informational setting. Unfortunately economics is singularly devoid of information theory, just as it is devoid of learning theory. One suspects that the "Homogeneous globule of self-interest," at which Veblen poked fun, not only is incapable of learning anything (because he knows everything already) but also is really incapable of "knowing" anything in the sense of receiving information. Jevons defined economics as "The mechanics of utility and self-interest," and as long as we stay with the maximization theory as a supposed theory of behavior, we are dealing with mechanical and not with informational or organizational systems. This is precisely why the maximization theory has been so unsatisfactory as a theory of behavior in spite of its virtues in other directions.

When we ask what we really mean by information, we are confronted with serious difficulties which no economist to date has even begun to face. Information is not a simple physical event such as a noise or a shape on a piece of paper. It is an event in a context. But the context is the thing that really determines the significance, or the information-content, of the event. One might define information as a hole in the middle of a lot of context were it not for the fact that the context itself consists of a lot of similar holes. The idea of a hole in the middle of a lot of holes boggles the human imagination. Nevertheless, this is the fantastic stuff of which language is made. A word is not so much a *thing* as a *place* in a sentence. If I shout, "Long live the X" the sentence derives its meaning only from its present day context. The letter X or another word in that particular sentence would have to mean, "Queen." I can make a set of noises in English and a different set of noises in Portuguese. To the physicist these are distinct and different phenomena but the information these different noises convey may be identical.

We cannot therefore look upon the executive as merely a kind of production function receiving sentences and paragraphs in his "In" box and grinding them into different sentences and paragraphs in his "Out" box in the manner of a mill grinding wheat into flour. A truer picture would be the executive as a "context" (or what the psychologists call a "body image"). This is the executive's picture of himself and his environment. The incoming information is a shot fired at this whole context. It results in a rearrangement—that is, a new picture—of where, and even who the executive is. The outgoing communications emanate from this entirely new picture. They are a function of the relation of this reorganized picture to the executive's role as he conceives it.

Suppose we raise the curtain on the chairman of the board of a large milling concern at five o'clock on a Friday afternoon just as he is leaving for home. He has in his mind a reasonably clear picture of how his company stands and what things it is doing. The picture, we assume, is a fairly rosy one and with a comfortable smile he prepares for an agreeable weekend of golf in the country. Then, his secretary hands him a telegram announcing that his largest mill has been burned to the ground. This information causes a radical readjustment

89

of his whole "body image" of his company. Where, a few moments ago he visualized a thriving mill he now visualizes a heap of ruins. It is obvious that the weekend is also ruined. Many new and unforseen decisions will have to be made. New information must be called for. How to satisfy promised deliveries? What is the state of the firm's insurance? How does this affect the firm's solvency? Can we meet the note that is due tomorrow? The decisions which are now taken flow not from the information directly but from the change in context which that information has produced.

Information, then, must be conceived not as a physical "thing" or configuration—the words on the paper or the noises in the ear—but as the whole rearrangement of the mental structures and pictures of the recipient under the impact of the "message"—i.e., the physical embodiment of the information. The act of "understanding" a particular message is the act of making the appropriate rearrangements of one's entire mental structure. Knowledge is not a mere pile of information to which further information is simply added. It is an organizational structure into which any new information has to be integrated. Information, then, is always a problem which has to be solved.

If we are ever to have a theory of economic behavior we must find some way of describing the mental structures or the knowledge of the executive. It must be a way of describing the impact of messages on this mental structure (that is, the way in which messages are turned

90

into information). We must also understand something about the learning process by which a succession of messages brings about cumulative changes in the mental structure. Perhaps a theory of economic behavior is simply a special case of a theory of behavior in general. Nevertheless, there is some possibility that the very limitations—and hence the simplicity—of the economist's abstraction may make it possible to develop models of economic behavior which are somewhat simpler than models of behavior in general and still throw a good deal of light on the general problem.

At this point I cannot elaborate on a theory that is yet to be born but I can illustrate the kinds of variables that might be involved. The mental structure of an executive will consist of three broad divisions: his memories of past events, his knowledge of present states, and his expectations of future events and states. The knowledge of the present and the expectations of the future must be derived ultimately from the memories of the past. The expectations of the future must be characterized by a degree of uncertainty—one that increases with the remoteness of the expectation in question. It is less often recognized that the knowledge of present states is also uncertain because of unavoidable imperfections in the information system. A great deal of the mental picture of the present state is *deduced* from messages received in the past and is deduced therefore with a degree of uncertainty.

I indicated previously that, even in the marginal

analysis, uncertainty is a powerful factor in explaining optimum positions in the short run. If uncertainty is undesirable efforts will be made to escape from it. This may be done by insurance, which is, in effect, the replacement of large uncertain losses by small certain losses (the premiums). It may also be done by liquidity. It is almost impossible to understand the asset-behavior of firms without introducing the idea of liquidity as an escape from uncertainty. The form of liquid assets can be changed easily in response to new information. Money is readily exchangeable in the market into many different kinds of assets. Assets may also be liquid in production—e.g., raw materials as opposed to manufactured products—and capable of being transformed in production into many different kinds of assets.

Uncertainty may also be avoided by manipulating and controlling the environment so that fewer variables are subject to uncertainty. Movements toward monopoly, toward control of buying or selling markets, toward defense in all its aspects, attempts to reduce the burden of uncertainty. Movements in the directions of ritualistic or self-justifying patterns of behavior might also fall in this category. However, these adjustments may not be profitable in the long run. They may lend the immediate comfort of the ostrich with its head in the sand but they do not provide intelligent adjustment to unforseen events. It is not the foolish, it is not the rigid, it is the meek (that is, the liquid and the adaptable) who are constantly inheriting the earth!

The mental structure of the executive consists of two parts. First, he has ideal values of the variables within his mental horizon. They are the balance sheet and income account items, prices, and general states of the world. The second part is his notion of actual values of these variables. The instructions he sends out are designed to reduce these homeostatic gaps and they depend in large measure on his perception of the nature of the effectors under his control. There is no use, obviously, in commanding the impossible. What is significant, however, is that in interpreting behavior, the messages the executive receives may result in radical readjustments of the ideal system of values as well as in readjustments in his perception of the real. These adjustments in the "ideal" system may be based on very small changes in information received and yet result in disproportionate effects on behavior. Frequently a message which is the culmination of a series is the straw that breaks the camel's back and radically overturns the ideal value structure.

Suppose, for instance, that a firm establishes a price policy for its distributors. It receives information that one of its distributors is cutting prices. Here is a divergence between the perception of the ideal and the real. The action will probably be to discipline the distributor and bring him into line. But suppose there is a succession of such messages. They could indicate the price has been set too high. On receiving the twentieth such message the whole price policy may be revised and a whole new set of instructions sent out. A single blast of the trumpet can bring down the walls of Jericho!

Again, in the light of the kind of theory outlined above, the economist might act as an adviser. The difficulty here is that the theory is an expectation rather than a reality and suffers from the uncertainty normally associated with all expectations! Nevertheless, this theory of organization and behavior, even in its present crude and unformed state, opens remarkable vistas of research *within the firm*. It is easy to suppose that in the next generation a research program in organization and communication may well be part of every forward-looking firm. Armed even with the simple apparatus outlined above the economist could ask some extremely important and penetrating questions. He might suggest in the first place that the organization of the firm be examined from the point of view of the *information system*. Most information systems are haphazard collections of traditional organizations and activities—accounting, which, if the truth must be known, is largely a by-product of the tax system and corporation law; labor relations, which is an offshoot of, or an attempt to avoid, union pressure; legal services, which are by-products of contractual relationships and the framework of regulatory laws; public relations, so frequently the results of the public relations of the public-relations men, plus a vast system of internal reports, time cards, disciplinary memoranda, telephone messages, lunches, gossip, golf, and informal relationships of all kinds.

Nobody, to my knowledge, has ever sat down in an actual or imaginary firm and asked himself whether this mass of information apparatus made any sense: does it result in the collection of a lot of information that is not necessary to intelligent action; does it fail to collect information that is necessary to intelligent action; what does anybody want to know anyway and is it worth the cost of finding out? Statistics has thrust its camel's nose into the tent of enterprise in the shape of quality control, market research, and various other sampling procedures. Accounting, for the most part, remains a legalistic and traditional practice, almost immune to self-criticism by scientific methods. And it is nobody's business to examine the communication-information problem as a whole, to examine how, in fact, the *messages* which chase each other all over an organization are translated into *information,* modifying ideal-structures, yielding new perceptions of homeostatic gaps, and so producing appropriate action.

The work of the industrial relations researchers has revealed the enormous gap which can exist between messages and information. The critical third organ— the orders-communicator—must not be conceived in merely verbal terms but in terms of a whole social relationship involving the impact of the mutual interaction of management, supervisory staff, and workers on the whole role-concept of individuals at all levels. It is well to remember Barnard's dictum that all authority proceeds from below upwards in the administrative hierarchy and not from above down! The basis of effective organization is the willingness of the lower echelons of a hierarchy to receive, understand, and carry out messages. And this frequently depends on the efficiency of the upward rather than on the downward channels of communication!

Another rewarding line of research would be the nature of the effectors. The ineffectiveness of organizational structures can frequently be traced to the lack of *selectivity* in the effectors. Instead of having each significant variable linked neatly to an effector of its own each effector is likely to affect many variables. Consequently the attempt to correct one homeostatic gap may lead to the creation of others. We fire off a blunderbuss to bring down a single bird and find that we have brought down a half dozen birds we had no intention of disturbing. Sometimes this is unavoidable, especially in view of the all-pervading influence of uncertainty.

> For all our scientific fuss
> Research is still a blunderbuss,
> We fire a monstrous charge of shot
> And sometimes hit, but mostly not!

The same caustic quatrain might be applied to a great many operations of top management where the ability to make several shots in the dark, in a number of different directions, still has a good deal of survival value.

Some of my readers may complain that this is all very well but it is not economics. If it is not, I reply, "So much the worse for economics." It may well be that the survival of mankind depends on our collective ability to solve the problem of world organization. If the economist can bring his skills to the understanding of economic organization that will be at least a step in the direction of salvation. And if people insist on calling this skill sociology, or even, what is a naughtier name, institutional economics, the *thing* is so important that it is worth a bad name!

The Economist's Vision of the Economy

CHAPTER IV

Political economy
May not be all it claims to be
But still, it can show up the tricks
Of uneconomic politics!

WHAT SPECIAL SKILLS of the economist contribute to the solution of problems of government in general, in particular, or even to world government? Here the economist encroaches upon the preserve of the political scientist. Nevertheless, government economic policy has been a traditional concern of the economist; taxation, tariffs, subsidies, government control or operation of industry, of the monetary system, and of financial institutions. There is no clear division between the economic problems and the non-economic problems of government although it might be claimed that the form and organization of government is the province of the political scientist whereas the economist occupies himself with the actions of government and their effects. This division leaves too much of the national defense in the domain of the economist who has never been happy with the study of an institution so inherently uneconomic. However, with the exception of the armed forces, it can fairly be claimed that all other transactions of government and most of its regulations fall within the purview of the economist.

What is the economist's picture of government as an organization or institution? Is it something like a firm, a giant corporation, or does it more nearly resemble a household? Or, is it neither, although possessing some characteristics of both firm and household in addition to marked peculiarities of its own? Conceived as an economic organization government has indeed many aspects of the firm. It takes in and pays out money. It gives out and takes in goods and services. It buys labor and innumerable commodities. It may also sell commodities. However, it differs from the firm in many important respects. It does not, for the most part, receive its money inflows, as a firm must, from the sale of goods and services to voluntary purchasers. By far the greater part of its receipts are derived from forced payment— taxation. It is a moot point in national income accounting whether these payments have in fact paid for anything—that is, whether government should be regarded as giving intangible services of some kind for its tax receipts. In most cases it is certainly difficult to identify *specific* services for which taxes are paid and it is probably wise to classify most taxes as payments for the overhead of society—that is, not allocable to any particular person, commodity, or enjoyment.

Another peculiarity of government, important in assessing its economic impact, is that generally it has no balance sheet and does very little asset accounting. Government accounts are usually drawn up on a strictly annual income basis. In this way government resembles a household since the capital accounts of most households are also apt to be haphazard. In theory, balance sheets may be drawn up for both households and government and we might, for instance, draw up a balance sheet for government in which the national debt was listed on the liabilities side and some corresponding item of "goodwill" or "capitalized taxable capacity" on the other. However, it would be most difficult to imagine any such item in government capital accounts as "net worth." For this reason, if for no other, it is impossible to apply the concept of profit maximization to government. Since profit is the growth of net worth, an institution without net worth obviously cannot adopt make-it-grow policies!

Nevertheless, the concepts of marginal analysis, in the wider sense of the maximization of a welfare function, are applicable to government. And even more, the concepts of economic behavior, developed from the theory of organization in the previous chapter, are especially applicable to government. From the point of view of marginal analysis the government can, in the formal sense, be regarded as a kind of household. It apportions its expenditures among many claimants—defense, education, research, social security, justice. This follows the general equimarginal principle that a household is supposed to follow in distributing expenditure for food, clothing, shelter and other basic necessities. There is an ideal distribution of expenditures. It is the distribution which it is not worth while to change out of the total which, being ideal, likewise is not worth while changing. As a principle this is undoubtedly true but it is too formal to be useful. In the case of the government, the formal maximization principle begs the most interesting question. It ignores the political process of give and take between different interests and groups. It is this give and take that ultimately determines the final budget. Nevertheless, it is useful merely to state a formal principle when there are some who do not believe it. The economist's duty is to raise his voice in defense of the proposition that *if resources are limited, what goes to one thing must be withdrawn from another.* Under widespread unemployment and with usable, but unused resources, the economist has an equal duty to proclaim that their use need not withdraw anything from anybody.

The more important principle in interpreting the economic behavior and impact of government is that of homeostasis and feedback outlined in the previous chapter. Regardless of a government's form or its objectives, there will be sensitive variables in its information system which create homeostatic gaps between an ideal value and a recorded value. In other words, there are certain signs of failure in the information which a government receives. These will spur the government to activity of some kind in an endeavor to remove the signs themselves. One important homeostatic variable is the feeling of military power or the sense of security. This is partly a function of the territorial ambitions of the country and partly the size of the military establishments of rival countries. Another important but rather vague variable is the internal popularity of the regime as reflected by elections, publications, newspapers, political activity and other manifestations of public opinion. The ideals of the party in power constitute another variable—or set of variables. This is the ideal body image of the state in the minds of those in power. Frequently these various homeostatic variables may be in conflict with one another; a government may seek popularity at the expense of its own ideals, or the almost perpetual tension in government between the desire to do a "good job" by its own standards may be at odds with the desire to perpetuate itself in power.

The theory of organization throws a good deal of light on the essential weakness of arbitrary and dictatorial regimes as compared with liberal and constitutional forms of government. The paradox of organizational structure is that the executive is dependent on his sources of information to make sound decisions whereas his sources of information may be dependent on him for their pay and position. Therefore the executive's informants may be more eager to tell him what they think he wants to know than to tell him what they know, or believe, to be the truth. Incidentally, this situation also exists within the firm. The executive depends for information on accountants and controllers who in turn are dependent on him. No doubt the device of the audit and the public accountant is an attempt to avoid this peril. However, the dictator has no such protection. He rules by fear and violence and surrounds himself with yes-men who keep their somewhat insecure positions by telling him only what will please him. Consequently he may find himself so insulated from the real world that his decisions relate only to the imaginary world of his biased information system; a situation inimical both to good government and to survival. The great case for liberty, even for dangerous liberty, is that without it there can be no adequate lines of communication between the government and the outside world. And the executive without communication is helpless; his power a mockery.

It would be too much to claim that the economists had a uniform concept of government. Political philosophies within the ranks of economists range from socialism to extreme laissez-faire. Nevertheless, it is possible to detect a certain cast of political conviction which flows from the skill of the economist. It arises from his concept of the social system as a system of general equilibrium. This is why both the economist and the ecologist hold similar views. The ecologist sees an *ecosystem* in nature as a complex, dynamic equilibrium of interacting populations of different species. The economist likewise sees society as a great pond or forest, filled with innumerable interacting species of economic and social organizations; gas stations, steel mills, automobiles, farms, food stores, wholesalers, stockbrokers, schools, churches, counties, states, and armies. In the midst of this forest stands the government. Ideally it is an agency representing the interests of the whole system. It operates on this complex system very much as a farmer or the forester modifies the natural ecosystem of the field or the woods; distorting the position of equilibrium by suppressing some species (weeds, criminals) and encouraging others (grain, useful industries) by various processes of seeding (education), harrowing (justice), fertilizing (subsidies), and scaring away the birds (protection).

The biological analogy must not be pressed too far. It merely emphasizes the interconnectedness of the system's variables as a warning against too much reliance on dealing with evils one at a time! Thus, if we are too successful in getting rid of one weed or pest we may find we have left ourselves exposed to more violent attacks by even worse weeds and pests which the eradicated weed had helped to suppress. The failure of prohibition in the United States is a good example of a failure to appreciate the complex ecological nature of the social system. Prohibition got rid of the open saloon but it gave rise to speakeasies and gangsters worse than the original pest! The biological analogy breaks down because government is not, or at least should not be, something alien to the culture in which it resides whereas the farmer is alien to his crops and livestock. Rather, government is an expréssion of the wills of the very people and institutions which it seeks to regulate. It is much as if a farm were to be governed by an assembly of cows, horses, and even rice and beans! Because of this, the problem of the *ends* of government—that is, the direction in which it seeks to distort the social ecosystem—is far from simple. Normally there are many conflicting ends, and the actual policies and behavior of governments vary according to which end, or which group within the society, is momentarily in a position to command attention and prestige.

There is a school of economists, ably represented by Professor Lionel Robbins in his *Nature and Significance of Economic Science,* which maintains that the economist, as such, is indifferent to ends and is concerned only with means. In practice it seems to be impossible, even for Professor Robbins, to maintain this extreme position. And no economist of any reputation has managed to construct an economics so bloodless as to be utterly indifferent to the ends of the system which it describes. All the great schools of economists—the mercantilists, the physiocrats, the classical economists, and the Keynesians—have had definite views on the objectives of economic life and policy. These views have both affected and been affected by the nature of the economic theories their protagonists espoused. It is therefore useful to spell out some of the objectives usually regarded by economists as important for economic policy. This is not because any one objective is paramount nor because the techniques of economic analysis guide the choice among them. It is because these possible objectives emerge from the economists' vision of social reality—or, if you will, from the nature of the economists' abstraction from social reality.

The first of these objectives is economic progress, or economic development, defined in terms of the rate of increase of real income per head. We recognize, of course, that all measures of real income are subject to the errors of aggregation. They are errors which become more serious in proportion to the diversity of the aggregates compared. Any comparison between real incomes in the United States for the year 1776 and the year 1957, or between the United States and China of today, is subject to wide error. Nevertheless, when the calculation shows that per capita income in China is, let us say $50 per annum, and in the United States is $1500 per annum, no amount of error in measurement can explain away the enormous difference nor eliminate the realities of economic progress and stagnation. It is possible that economists and economic statisticians have made governments increasingly sensitive to the rate of economic progress as one of the most significant variables of the system.

If nobody knows whether an economy is progressing,

106

stagnating, or regressing, except through vague half-memories of a golden past, nobody is likely to worry about it or try to speed up the rate of development. However, where the availability of economic information makes politicians and people in general *aware* of their rate of economic progress and especially of their own rate *relative* to higher rates elsewhere, their attention is concentrated on the problem. For instance, the British people and government are increasingly aware of the growing gap between British and American standards of living. This is mainly due to the differential rates of economic progress. Income per capita in the two countries was about equal in the early years of the twentieth century. The differential, now so noticeable, is the result of a two-to-three per cent per annum rate of growth of the American per capita income as opposed to a one-to-two per cent per annum rate of growth in Britain. The rate is averaged over the last fifty years. Countries like India are becoming acutely conscious of their relative positions in the economic world and of the rate of change in their per capita incomes. Actually, some of them may have to exert all their efforts merely to prevent a decline rather than achieve a positive rate of growth.

If the rate is unsatisfactory it is unfortunately easier to measure progress than to know what to do about it. Economic development is a fruit of the whole culture of a region and cannot be isolated from the rest of the culture. Therefore, at the point of actual policy, economics as such offers little guidance. Historically it would seem that a variety of cultures and institutions are capable of stimulating rapid rates of economic growth and an even greater variety are capable of suppressing it. In a puritan, protestant culture the typical institutions of capitalism—free markets, developed financial institutions, financial markets, and a minimum of government "overhead" devoted to education, transportation, security of person and security of property, have been very successful in promoting rapid rates of economic development. In other cultures, as in Latin America, similar capitalist institutions have been less successful in promoting balanced and steady growth. In a culture like China's the same institutions have been outright failures whereas in Japan's they are a considerable success. The centrally planned economy of Soviet Russia produced a rapid rate of economic growth although at a tremendous cost in human life, freedom and dignity. The ancient, centrally planned, non-market economies of Egypt and Peru, as far as we know, produced a stationary or even retrogressive society. It is evident that the answer to the question: "What can a government do to increase a 'too low' rate of economic development?" is one which an economist cannot answer by himself.

There are of course some things which an economist does know about economic progress, and Professor Nurkse has said them all!

There must be capital accumulation and there must be a reorganization of agriculture production to release

108

workers from agriculture. There must be investment in the "cultural overhead"—in the basic skills of literacy, of elementary science and mechanics, of the ability to replace traditional knowledge with scientific knowledge. There must also be investment in the physical overhead —the means of transportation, schools, and the like. There must be a *balanced development* leading to external economies and the growth of internal markets. Even this skeletal, theoretical structure should be an important guide to governments seeking to find the missing elements in the structure of their economies.

There is still another broad area in which economists have exercised a good deal of influence on the objectives of government policy. This is the area of income distribution. Economists, at least from the time of Adam Smith, have had a strong equalitarian bent. No doubt this arises, at least in part, out of the *rights of man* philosophies of the eighteenth century. It is also a consequence of the nature of the economist's abstraction. When the focus of interest is commodities then *man* becomes a mechanical force pushing commodities around and one such mechanical man is exactly like another. Economic men are bound to be equal because they are all equally abstract from the rich complexities and varieties of flesh-and-blood human nature. This abstraction is epitomized in Marx whose social universe is a world of real commodities populated by totally unreal (and equal) people. But if we have a universe of abstract, and therefore uniform individuals, it follows that their preference functions are all alike and it follows further that the social utility of the mass is maximized when all incomes are equal. Under these assumptions redistributing income from the rich to the poor will always benefit the poor more than it harms the rich because the marginal utility of the dollar is always greater for a person of lower income than for a person of higher income. On the other hand we can retain the principle that the marginal social utility of the dollar should be equal for all persons and still find this position consistent with unequal incomes. That is, we can do this as long as those whose marginal utility curves decline slowest get the most income. However, it is argued that because of the interpersonal incomparability of utilities it is impossible to know *which* people should have the higher income. Consequently the only practicable rule, in the face of ignorance, is that of equality. The fact that an individual with the wit of Bernard Shaw and another with the technical ability of A. P. Lerner should apparently have believed this nonsense is a remarkable tribute to the proposition that one should never underestimate the power of an abstraction.

In spite of the absurdity of the extreme position, the degree of inequality which an unrestrained market economy is likely to produce, clearly violates the sense of justice of a democratic society and the sense of brotherhood of a Christian one. No man but an utter swine could gorge himself with food at one end of his table while his children starved at the other end. Simi-

110

larly, in a society profoundly affected by the Christian idea of the universal family of mankind, the conscience of society will never be at ease as long as the rich waste food and clothing while their brothers the poor go hungry and naked. In virtually all modern societies the state has felt obliged to take measures to redistribute income, to relieve the necessities of the poor, and to curb the economic power of the rich.

The economist cannot say exactly what the ideal distribution of income should be. Nor can he be sure of the extent to which particular measures will change the distribution of income among persons or among the functional shares of wages, rent, and profit. We are reasonably sure that a progressive income tax is a powerful instrument for affecting the final personal distribution of income. Some of its effects on salaries, particularly in the case of scarce and expensive talent, may be avoided by raising the before-tax income. On the other hand, most large incomes are due to aggregations of property. The only way in which the progressive nature of the tax can be avoided is to break up concentrations of property which, after all, will tend to equalize incomes anyway. Whatever the theoretical considerations the statistical evidence for the redistribution of income by progressive taxation is overwhelming.

It is less clear that measures taken to change the functional distribution among wages, rent, and profit have been successful. For instance, the proportion of

111

national income going to labor has shown little if any long-run tendency to rise in spite of the rise of the labor movement in the United States. In the period of great increase in union membership, from 1933 to 1943, the proportion of national income going to wages actually fell. Indeed, it would seem that the functional shares are much more dependent on the monetary movements of inflation and deflation than they are on any conscious policies. The effect of inflation, especially in reducing the proportion of national income going to rent and interest and in increasing the proportion going to profits, is certainly unintended and merely a by-product of different policy objectives.

The skill of the economist clearly reveals the importance of examining potential relationships between redistribution and progress. Up to a point, redistribution is likely to be an aid to progress especially when the redistribution is away from an idle, tradition-centered, rentier class toward the active profit-makers and the workers. In so far as redistribution can raise the consumption function in a period of depression it likewise helps to remove underconsumption as an obstacle to economic development. There must be some point, however, beyond which the attempt to redistribute income destroys the incentive to innovate and penalizes investment, thus leading to a decline in the rate of economic development. This is always a high price to pay even for the lowest income groups. Although they may benefit temporarily through redistribution the time

112

comes when they would be better off had they received a smaller share of a more rapidly growing income. We cannot say that a given degree of redistribution is always associated with a given change in the rate of economic progress because the relationship depends on the way in which the redistribution is accomplished. For instance, there is no evidence that the personal redistribution, which has taken place in the United States in the past twenty years, has in any way resulted in a slackening in the rate of economic progress. If anything, the reverse has been the case, for record rates of economic growth and investment have been achieved in recent years. The same is perhaps even more true of Canada. One is less sure of Britain although even there the unsatisfactory rate of economic growth is a complex phenomenon which may have little or nothing to do with the degree of equality of income achieved. Nevertheless, even in the United States, one suspects that if there had not been a redistribution of income toward profit and away from interest and rents, the personal redistribution, by itself, might have had unfavorable results.

The economist has a good deal to say about another very important objective of government economic policy. This is the broad objective of economic stabilization. This has two different, though not unrelated, aspects. The first is the stabilization of the price level or of the value of money. The second is the stabilization of output and employment. The latter is perhaps the more important problem, especially from the point of view of the success or failure of government policy. People complain when there is inflation and a high cost of living but they rebel and revolt when there is mass unemployment and agricultural depression. By stabilization of output and employment we do not mean the maintenance of output and employment at a stationary level. What we really mean is the maintenance of an orderly rate of growth uninterrupted by periods of stagnation or decline.

It is no exaggeration to say that the past twenty years have brought a great increase in understanding the problem of depression. At the very least it should result in a corresponding increase in the ability to take intelligent measures to prevent it. There has been no real test of the new knowledge because conditions have not been ripe for a major depression. If such a depression were to occur it is not certain that governments would have the skill and understanding to apply the new knowledge. But the economist is confident he has something that is well worth applying.

The development of a cumulative body of national income statistics, as well as the development of the Keynesian and post-Keynesian theoretical structures, has done a great deal to reveal the broad *dimensions* of the problem. It is abundantly clear, for instance, that the old dispute between the underconsumption and the underinvestment theories of the business cycle is resolved in the realization that both are correct. Unemployment generally means there is not enough consumption *and* investment (willing accumulation) added together to maintain a full employment output. The general lines of the policies that should be employed are clear from the diagnosis. An increase in disposable income, relative to gross national product (through, for instance, reducing taxes and running a cash budget deficit) will raise the consumption function. Government investment in public works can help take up the slack in aggregate investment as also will suitably designed tax incentives for private investment. Monetary policy can be geared to monetary expansion through low interest rates, easy central bank credit, and other devices. If this can be done without creating an atmosphere unfavorable to the morale of private enterprise so much the better. Indeed, it may be that the best safeguard against depression is radical policies carried out by conservative governments!

Politically the stabilization of the price level may turn out to be more difficult than the prevention of depression, although the broad lines of the economics of the problem are clear. Inflation is almost universally a symptom of "over-consumption" or "over-absorption"— a situation in which society is trying to consume and accumulate more than it can produce even at full employment. Such a situation will result in inventory shortages and, even in the absence of any increase in the quantity of money, the price level will rise because of the shortage of commodity stocks. There may be, for instance, a boom in the construction of fixed capital which withdraws resources from the production of current output but contributes to money incomes. The usual source of inflation is withdrawal of resources from current output by government, generally for military purposes, without an adequate tax system by which disposable incomes may be reduced proportionately to the reduction in available output. In either case, if the money supply is flexible and elastic, as it is in all but the most primitive economics, a rise in prices is likely to call forth an increased money supply to sustain and even augment the inflationary process. Thus, in the case of a non-government inflation, set off by an excess of private construction of fixed capital, this same construction will be financed in part by bank loans which in turn lead directly to an increase in the total of bank deposits. If the rise in prices of inventories of circulating capital is proportionally greater than the decline in their physical quantities—and this is frequently the case—the value of inventories will rise in spite of the decline in their physical volume and new bank loans may be made to finance the increase in inventory values.

Government inflation is the direct result of inadequate tax collections. If there is a cash budget deficit—that is, if what the government pays out to all recipients is less than what it takes in from all sources—the direct result will be an equal increase in the money stocks of the people. Thus, if government takes in $9,000,000 and pays out $10,000,000 in a certain time period it is evident that the money stocks of the people will have grown as a direct consequence by $1,000,000. This growth in private money stocks may be augmented or it may be counteracted by inducing movements in the private banking system but the direct effect is clear. An initial rise in prices—perhaps even of a purely speculative nature—involving a decline in the demand for money, or a rise in the velocity of circulation, is likely to increase the cash deficit of government. The reason is that government expenditures are sensitive to the current price level and tend to fluctuate in total volume with it. On the other hand government receipts tend to be more closely related to the price level of some months, or even years, past. In this connection it is interesting to note that the development of pay-as-you-go taxes has perceptibly improved the ability of the tax system to counteract inflation. This ability is accentuated by the progressive tax on income: a rise in the money income of society automatically increases the proportion of income which is paid in taxes. Such a tax system is an automatic safeguard against hyper-inflation. Money income rises under the impact of inflation, tax collections become a larger and larger proportion of national income, and soon everyone invades what used to be the upper income brackets so that eventually the government runs a cash surplus sufficient to stop the inflation.

In a period of genuine over-absorption, whether caused by high investment in fixed capital or by war, it is not enough merely to have a balanced budget to prevent inflation. It is necessary to have a budget surplus. An over-absorption situation is one in which the incomes generated by the overall output of the system are so high that the amount of current output, which society is willing and able to consume, is greater than the maximum amount of current output available for consumption. If this situation is not to result in an upward movement in prices—a movement which may have to go a long way before it is self-correcting—there must be a reduction in disposable income sufficient to bring the purchases of current output into equality with available production. This means generally that money must actually be withdrawn from private money stocks by increasing tax collections until the government has a cash surplus. It is not difficult to see why wars, especially major wars, inevitably result in inflation. It is too much to expect of any government that it should run a cash surplus at a time when it is multiplying its expenditures!

The major impact of inflation is its effect on the distribution of assets and income. Inflation of course shifts that distribution away from those with fixed assets and incomes toward those with asset and income values that follow the rising price level. Consequently the shift is away from the rentier, the pensioner, and the official towards the profit maker, the entrepreneur and the farmer. Inflation itself tends to correct the over absorption which caused it in so far as it injures *low savers* who consume more than they produce and benefits the *high savers* who produce more than they consume. This however, involves a social cost. There are wide redistributions of wealth over which there is no conscious control nor about which there has been any public discussion. One's sense of fair play and justice is aroused when it is realized that frequently those really injured are the widows and orphans, the retired, the salaried and professional classes and charitable institutions. In contrast the beneficiaries of inflation are often the rich or at least those with economic power. Inflation therefore may run strongly counter to equalitarian policies.

There is an even more subtle social cost in the possible destruction of the organization of finance. In a society which is unaccustomed to inflation and has not adapted its financial institutions to the expectation of long run inflation, inflation then means the reduction of real rates of interest to very low or even to negative levels. Let us suppose rates of interest are about 5 per cent per annum and the annual rate of increase of prices is about 8 per cent. A man who lends $100.00 at the beginning of the year will get back 105 nominal dollars at the end of the year. But, in terms of purchasing power, the $105.00 will only be worth 97 of the beginning-of-the-year dollars. In real terms his capital has shrunk by $3.00 and the real rate of interest is therefore minus 3 per cent per annum. If this state of affairs goes on for very long either people will become unwilling to lend (i.e., to hold contractual assets) or else nominal rates of interest will rise to cover the expected rise in the price level. This, in fact, seems to be what happened in Brazil.

Both of these results may have unfortunate long run consequences. Debt performs a real function in society in that it enables people to separate ownership from the control of real capital. If debt disappears it means that already existing and profitable institutions are given a strong advantage while the youthful, beginning enterprise suffers a corresponding disadvantage. Inflation underscores the well-worn comment that to him that hath shall be given. Old, established firms find it easier to survive while youthful firms with ideas, but no capital, find it difficult to break into the economy on borrowed money. The function of the rate of interest and the function of the institution of credit and debt, as factors in economic development, require much research before they are understood well enough for purposes of practical application. It is possible, however, that just as development may be hampered by too high rates of interest and prohibitive costs of borrowing, development may also be hampered by too low rates of interest (in real terms) and an inadequate supply of funds.

If this problem is solved by raising the nominal rates of interest to allow for depreciation of the monetary unit, that solution may be satisfactory as long as the inflation continues. However, should the inflation end, followed by deflation, then the burden of interest become absurdly high. Therefore, where money rates of interest have been forced up by inflation, a society may find itself committed to continuing inflation and unable to stabilize the price level.

Whether a society should try to stabilize its long run price level or learn to adapt its institutions to long run inflation is a moot question. There are many indications that the institutions of capitalism have been developing along lines which make it much easier to run an economy under the gentle pressure of a little inflation. The organization of the economy into economic interest groups such as labor unions, farm organizations, cartels, and business associations, may not affect the distribution of income as much as it does the rigidity of the price structure. It is increasingly difficult to adjust any particular price downward because of resistance from those groups directly affected. Any one of these groups is prepared to fight the reduction of the price of its own product. It is less ready to resist a price rise of all other products in spite of the fact that the effect on its terms of trade is just the same. Thus, labor resists a cut in money wages as a direct action of the employer—something labor understands and can fight. It doesn't resist, because it doesn't know how, a rise in the cost of living which, by reducing real wages, accomplishes exactly the same thing. Like the weather, the price level is an impersonal thing over which we feel we have no control. In contrast, we feel we do have control over the immediate price of labor, farm products, industrial products, or whatever commodity provides our money

121

income. Consequently in deflation there are strong resistences to the fall of particular prices or wages. Therefore deflation is apt to take the form of a decline in output and employment rather than a decline in prices and money wages.

The deflationary solution to the problem of under-absorption would be analogous to the inflationary solution to the problem of over-absorption. A general fall in prices and money wages shifts income toward the rentiers, the pensioners, and all those who are injured by inflation. If this group is a low saving group the shift in the distribution of income, as a result of a fall in the price-wage level, would cause the consumption function to rise. If this went far enough it would eventually yield full employment. Practically, however, this is impossible because of the institutional inflexibility of prices and money wages in the downward direction. There isn't as much inflexibility in the upward direction but the continuing organization of society into economic pressure groups may introduce upward as well as downward rigidities in the price-wage structure. For instance, in a period of rapid inflation the wages of unorganized labor rise faster than the wages of organized labor. This is mainly because organized labor has difficulty in renegotiating its complicated contracts while the easy verbal revisions of unorganized labor are done on the spot. Downward inflexibility in a highly organized society is so great that industrial and agrarian strife is an almost certain result. For example, in Britain and the United States the *correction* of the various war inflations, especially the 1815, 1865, and 1919 peaks, was accomplished only at a grave cost in unemployment and social disorder. With increasing organization and rigidity in society deflation becomes almost impossible. If this is true, inflation can never be corrected and a long-run inflationary bias is introduced into the economy.

I have presented these considerations in some detail because they illustrate the way in which an economist thinks. His mental picture is that of the economy as a whole; its entire surface disturbed by successive waves of inflation or deflation, progress or retrogression, creating income and economic power shifts that result from these great, impersonal movements of the whole rather than from the particular plans of particular individuals. Because of his approach to the problems of economic policy the economist is far more likely to perceive relationships and even solutions that would never occur to the individual who looks at one thing at a time.

An example of great political importance in the United States is the problem of parity in agriculture. An economist describes this as a problem of the *terms of trade* of agriculture. The parity ratio is the ratio of the prices of things the farmer sells to the prices of the things the farmer buys. As a parenthetical comment, we have here an interesting example of the way in which a development in the information system has a profound influence on policy and behavior. Parity would undoubtedly never become a political issue had it not been developed as a statistical concept and its value calculated by the Bureau of Agricultural Economics! The terms of trade of American agriculture were low between 1920 and 1940 as compared to the period of 1909-1914; a period that later came to be regarded as the *ideal*. The farmer and the farm politician consider this a matter of "justice in distribution"—that is, the demand of the farmer for a larger share of the national income. To them it is a problem of "doing something for agriculture." This means subsidies, crop restriction programs, dumping surpluses abroad, price supports, credit facilities, encouragement of cooperatives, government purchases, government insurance, and on down the line of what is generally looked upon as agricultural policy.

The economist's vantage point, his vision of the economy as a whole, permits him to look at the problem very differently. He recognizes the agricultural problem as not being a problem of agriculture at all! To illustrate: he knows there are good reasons for the disadvantageous position of agriculture. A long-run cause rests, paradoxically enough, on the continual decline of resources engaged in agriculture when agriculture is technically progressive. This is true because of the inelastic demand for most agricultural products as *necessities*. The result of technical progress in agriculture is a relative shift of resources out of agriculture into industry. However, the only way to move resources is to squeeze them—that is, make the declining industry less

124

attractive than the expanding industry. In a market economy this is accomplished through the price system and the terms of trade. Technical improvements in agriculture will therefore cheapen agricultural commodities in relation to others until enough resources have been attracted away from agriculture to restore the balance.

In a society in which the techniques of agriculture are improving, with output per man increasing rapidly, the migration from agriculture may never catch up to the requirements of progress and consequently agriculture may seem to be constantly depressed. The remedy is not to prevent the migration from agriculture by subsidizing it but to encourage the migration so the benefits of agricultural progress may be enjoyed by the farmers as well as the rest of us. These benefits will take the form of a larger volume of industrial products. Within the structure of agriculture itself the same process applies. An improvement in methods of corn production should be reflected in an increased output of steak and strawberries rather than an increased consumption of corn pone.

Industrial depression is also a cause of unfavorable terms of trade in agriculture. The terms of trade of agriculture are roughly the ratio of what goes out from agriculture to what comes in to agriculture. What goes out is the *agriculture surplus*—that is, the food the agricultural population produces but does not eat. What goes in is the *industrial surplus*—that is, the products

125

that industry does not absorb in its own consumption and accumulation. In a depression agricultural *production* does not decline and may even increase slightly. The agricultural surplus, that which is sold by farmers, may likewise increase. The farmer's response to hard times is to eat less and work harder. On the other hand, as industrial production declines sharply so does the industrial surplus. Thus the farmer is exchanging *more* agricultural product for *less* industrial product than before—that is, the parity ratio, or his terms of trade, has deteriorated. But is plain that the real reason has nothing to do with agriculture—it is the decline in *industrial* production which leads to the deterioration of the farmer's position. The solution to the problem cannot be found within agriculture alone. It must be found in a general solution to the problem of depression.

Even though the vision of the economist is that of the economy as a whole, he must be constantly aware of the dangers of too much aggregating and averaging. He insists upon looking for the significant—that is, the homogeneous—aggregates in the economy, and warns against thinking of aggregates as homogeneous which are really heterogeneous.

Agriculture again provides an excellent example. Statistics are frequently cited to show that agriculture is at a disadvantage because its per capita income is much lower than that of the industrial population. Aid to agriculture is therefore advocated on the basis of this information. When examined closely it will be found

126

that agriculture is not a homogeneous industry. It consists of at least two entirely different sections: a commercial section in which incomes are reasonably comparable to those of industry and a subsistence section in which incomes are very low indeed. There is practically no justification therefore for aid to agriculture as a whole for the simple reason that agriculture is not a whole. Poverty in agriculture, especially in times of industrial full employment, is almost entirely a problem of subsistence agriculture. Here the difficulty is not so much the low price of the product as it is the low volume of production.

This is true even in a country as generally rich as the United States where there are still some two million farmers, mostly in the South and mountain country, whose low level of production accounts for most of the low average income of agriculture. Unfortunately agricultural policy, designed to support prices, helps the rich farmer more than it does the poor farmer. Here is a curious deficiency in our information system. Agriculture has obtained a sympathetic hearing in its claims for support because of its low average incomes. The poor farmers, however, whose low incomes bring down the average, have benefited very little from the policies designed to raise agricultural incomes. Because we have thought of "helping agriculture" rather than of "helping the poor" we have actually used the poverty of the poor to justify policies which have in effect subsidized the rich.

The points I have made illustrate the view and attitude the economist brings to problems of government. It is not the legal view concerned with the niceties of language and procedure. It is not the view of the political scientist interested in power struggles, the processes of legislation, and the procedures of administration. It is not the view of the politician interested in what will sound well in speeches and what will impress a constituent. All these have their place and a government by economists is not to be thought of. It would never come down from the clouds. But government without economists, or at least without the vision and the ideas of the economists, is a sad affair. It then becomes a blind beast plunging madly in response to pricks and jabs which it can neither avoid nor understand.

It is the peculiar skill of the economist to bring to government a clear image of its function as a *governor*, or control mechanism. He sees government's task, for instance, as that of stabilizing the wild gyrations of the free market without destroying its essential freedom. He sees it as promoting economic progress, correcting economic injustices, and defending personal liberties where there is a perceived divergence between the image of the ideal and the perception of the real. To these ends the economist develops an information system—price levels, national income statistics, and so on—by which the mind of the decision maker can grasp the essential dimensions of the social and economic scene. This information system is like the thermometer of a thermostat or the dials and instruments of the aviator, without which control systems would not be possible. The theoretical system of the economist then points to the *effects* of government action and gives at least qualitative clues as to what actions produce what effects.

If the head of any non-communist government were to ask his economist advisers what to do about inflation, or about a depression, and even in a smaller degree about economic development, he will get much the same answers. There will be local variations and individual differences but by and large economists speak the same language and give much the same kind of advice no matter where they are. This is evidence that the skill of the economist is more than verbal, and as the economist contemplates the increasing role which he and his confreres play in government, he may be allowed perhaps a thimbleful of pardonable pride. No more than a thimbleful—for there is a sad record of mistakes. Most economists, for instance, thought that there was going to be great unemployment after the end of the Second World War. There wasn't. However, we are pretty sure *why* there wasn't and even wisdom after the event is not complete foolishness. There is a real contrast between the kind of advice a government gets from its economists and the kind it gets from its international relations experts. Economists operate in a world in which at least the main outlines of the landscape are now visible and in which the main instruments of control are known. In the vital matter of war and peace

we still operate by lights and flashes, hunches and in-
stincts; we have no adequate theoretical system and no
adequate instruments of control.

Trade—Not Aid for the Sciences

CHAPTER V

Unless exchange is many-sided
In vain is labor subdivided.
This principle applies, we find
To all the products of the mind

IT HAS BEEN SAID, no doubt by a cynic, that when a man
has nothing more to say on his own subject he turns to
the integration of the sciences. In spite of the dangers of
venturing into other specialists' fields I confess to a
strong interest in the integration of knowledge. This is
not that I have exhausted my interest in my own field
of specialization but because the pursuit of any problem
in economics always draws me into some other science
before I can catch it. Am I interested in the theory of
the firm? The basic problems of behavior, and therefore
of economic behavior, seem to lie in sociology, psychology, or even physiology. Am I interested in the theory

of economic development? This problem is a cultural one and seems to lie in cultural anthropology or sociology. Am I interested in wages? Again my interest will lead me to sociology or social psychology. For some years I have been forced, almost against my will, into an interest in the other social sciences because the real problems refused to stay within the neat compartments of academic specialization.

This has led me to conduct a seminar in the Integration of the Social Sciences. Within the seminar I have brought together many specialists from many disciplines to work on some problem of mutual interest. For example, during one year the theory of competition and cooperation underwent a careful examination by biologists, economists, sociologists and social psychologists. During another year the theory of behavior and organization was studied with the aid of examples ranging from unicellular organisms to the Federal Reserve System. A third year was devoted to the theory of growth—in the crystal, the cell, the body, the building, the personality, the community, the firm, the economic system, and the language. A fourth year was spent on the theory of information and communication, bringing together contributions from electrical engineers, physiologists, psychologists, and sociologists. A fifth year was given over to the theory of conflict—in international relations, in arms races, in industrial relations, in the family, within the personality.

From the experience in these seminars I have built

132

the strong conviction that there is far more unity in knowledge than is generally realized. The confinement of scholars to the narrow cells of their specialties has obscured the broad patterns common to all. Knowledge is a many-storied building where there is poor elevator service between floors and each discipline occupies a different floor. The floor plans on all levels are much alike in spite of a balcony here and a recess there. Some things are rather clear in the design of some floors which are not as clear on others. The reason for availing oneself of the occasional elevator is that most of the basic phenomena of the empirical world are to be found in *all* sciences—behavior, interaction, growth, and decay. Certain phenomena, only too apparent in one science, may exist in an obscure and less comprehensible form in other sciences. No man should expect to be thoroughly familiar with any discipline other than his own. Nevertheless, even a cursory acquaintance with the other floors of the building may lead him to investigate corners and closets of his own floor which he never suspected were there.

In the course of the integration seminar it became evident that the elevators run both ways. It has sometimes been argued that the origin of all science is physics and that if we knew everything about the physical world we should know everything there is to know. Quite apart from the metaphysical question of the reality of non-physical universes and systems, it is not an accurate description of the relationship among

133

the sciences to suggest that borrowing can take place only from the ground up. It is true that the physical sciences developed first and their concepts have profoundly influenced all those developed later. Nevertheless the economist should recall that next to physics his is the oldest of the theoretical sciences. Even though the evolution of its empirical phase has taken many years, the essential framework of theoretical economics, as well as an understanding of what constitutes an economic system, were described in the writings of Adam Smith in 1776. This antedated the success of chemistry in disentangling itself from the coils of the Phlogiston Theory. Economics was recognized long before the other social and biological sciences appeared on the horizon. In a way it is fair to say that economics was the parent of scientific biology, since Darwin acknowledged his basic indebtedness to Malthus for the idea of natural selection. It could also be claimed that the theory of ecological succession is to be found in Adam Smith's magnificent, but little read, discussion of the changes which take place in the species (commodities) that inhabit the economic universe as society progresses.

I think it is quite likely that we are entering an era of much more interaction among the sciences if only for the reason that each science is becoming better integrated within its own boundaries. It can now afford to offer and accept contributions from other sciences without fear of a threat to its inner integrity. What is more, it is likely that the social sciences, now undergoing rapid development in their ability to perceive and interpret their respective universes, will be able to offer suggestions and contributions to the biological and physical sciences. The social sciences have been slower to develop than the physical sciences not only because the latter offered quicker returns but also because the universes of the social scientist are less uniform and regular. Consequently the social sciences are more susceptible to sampling error. The social scientist is less able to use the experimental method, not only because his materials (subjects) resist in a way that atoms and cells do not, but also because the experimental method is only valid in an investigative universe so uniform as to eliminate the sampling problem.

The chemist is fairly well convinced that a hydrogen atom in Moscow is exactly like a hydrogen atom in Washington and therefore any old hydrogen atom he meets anywhere will serve his purposes equally well. The social scientist has no such illusions about men, nor for that matter about hydrogen when the latter is either a commodity or a weapon! He labors under still another difficulty; he cannot investigate his universe without changing it. Once a man has answered a questionnaire he is no longer the same man. *If* people believe an economist's prediction, the event he predicted may come true simply *because* he predicted it. If astronomers had to deal with stars that got angry and refused to shine when an astronomer looked at them, or if atoms felt as strongly about physicists as physicists do about atoms, or if a cell blushed with embarrassment every time it caught the eye of a bacteriologist, the natural and biological scientists would then be caught in a rat-maze similar to the one that frustrates the social scientist.

Nevertheless, the social scientist has certain advantages. The very difficulties of his universe have forced him to face questions which exist only in more tenuous form in the other sciences. Thus, even the physicist now has to face the difficulty created when the observer is an important part of the universe which he is observing, or where the act of observation changes the universe to be observed. The Heisenberg principle of indeterminancy is an example of this difficulty. Nils Bohr has suggested that a similar difficulty may plague the biologist: that the attempt to discover the physical substratum of life will always be frustrated because the very act of investigating the living substance kills it.

But the social scientist is at an advantage as well as a disadvantage in being a part of the universe he is investigating. The physicist has never been an atom and cannot have much notion of what it is like to be one. The biologist has never been a single cell or a plant although, on occasion, he can be very much an animal. On the other hand the sociologist has usually been in a family, the economist has frequently been in a firm, and the psychologist is as capable of thought, perception, and emotion as his subjects. This intimacy gives the social scientist a certain inside track denied to his fellow scientists. Even so, it is often a dangerous track to run on. It is even avoided altogether by those very pure-minded social scientists who consider it undignified and unsporting to take advantage of being an insider.

There are examples of areas in which economics can throw light on phenomena that are fairly clear in the universe of the economist but have rather less clear analogues in the universes of other sciences. These suggestions, if they have value, must be examined critically by those who are expert in the relevant fields. In this essay they must be taken as flights of the imagination rather than sober and settled propositions. Pigou once said that we do economics because it is fun, and I offer these suggestions in somewhat the same spirit. I commend first to the sociologists, therefore, the idea that a generalized balance sheet and a transformation function are applicable in some degree to all organizations. I suspect there is a good deal of confusion in all social sciences between transformation functions and welfare or preference functions. It might be a disciplinary experience for all sciences to go through something like the rise (and perhaps the collapse) of welfare economics.

Writing in the social sciences tends to be shot through with the authors' *implicit* preference functions which never quite get out into the open. For example, the whole idea of "health," and particularly the idea of mental health, is full of implicit and cloudy preference functions. How do we know, for instance, that creativeness in the human organism is not in part a function of what the physician and the psychiatrist stigmatizes as

137

ill health? Or again, do we really want people to be well-adjusted in a society like ours? Are there limits in human decency to the development of the science of human relations? Is there a danger of psychology degenerating into the study of how to win friends and influence people, or even worse, how to push people around and make them like it? What are the essential variables of sociological and psychological systems anyway? What is success in marriage? Can we draw a balance sheet for a family in as many dimensions as we wish, and is there any sense in trying to reduce this to a single dimension of success? Where are the significant transformation functions in the sociological and psychological variables? How much of X do I have to give up in order to get a unit of Y, and what are X and Y (frustration, aggression, love, hate, conflict, reconciliation, power, affection)?

When you reduce a multidimensional aggregate to a linear scale, as you do in scaling and testing, what determines the coefficients of valuation—or do you take the first numbers that come into your head? Where in sociological and psychological interaction are there things that look like exchange (metabolism)? What are the dimensions of *growth*—of the personality, of the family, of the church, of the social group, of learning, of social integration? What *accumulates* in the sociological and psychological systems that corresponds to the economist's notion of capital; what is produced and consumed; what is the *nutrition* of the group or the personality? These are questions that come to the mind of the economist as he looks at the non-economic aspects

138

of social reality. They are not necessarily the questions a sociologist or a psychologist asks, but to the economist they are worth asking because the structure of thought of economics has applications far beyond the abstractions of the universe of commodities.

Let me illustrate by an example of the application of the economist's scheme of thought to an applied field— the field of labor relations. It is a highly composite one; half sociology, a large part psychology, a smaller part economics, with dashes of law, engineering, anthropology and even ethics. The economist's approach to the industrial relationship is to look upon labor as a commodity—and so it is, in spite of the protests of the International Labor Organization and the declaration of the Clayton Act. Obviously, it is much more than a commodity, but then so is every commodity. The real question is what understanding of the industrial relationship can be gained by focusing attention on labor in its *aspect* as a commodity and what can only be understood by focusing attention on other elements in the relationship. I was once appointed to an academic committee charged with the responsibility of establishing a program in labor relations. One of my fellow members was a psychiatrist. I spent the whole year of meetings trying, unsuccessfully, to persuade him that economics had something to contribute to the study of the labor relationship. In his mind the labor problem was bounded by the love life of foremen and the neuroses of workers.

The economist's bailiwick, within the labor problem,

is of course the theory of wages. This is not to suggest that he shines in explaining why wages in one plant are so different from wages for similar jobs in another plant just across the road. If, however, one asks why money wages doubled in the United States from 1939 to 1949, or why wages are higher in the United States than they are in Brazil, then the economist is the only person who can explain. Within their own particular disciplines the psychologist and the sociologist would never spot the relationship between rising wages and war finance, between relative wages and relative scarcities of capital; and no amount of talk about group morale, or neuroses, or personnel management will ever answer those questions.

The major concern at this point, however, is not so much the economist's contribution to the narrower problems of wages as it is his contribution of a frame of reference to those problems which lie within the provinces of the sociologist and the psychologist. For instance, the economist can point out that most of the elements in the total industrial relationship can be expressed in terms of the exchange relationship. In this relationship the worker gives up something. He gives up time. He also gives up the alternative uses of time in other work, or time for leisure. He likewise gives up energy, the psychic satisfactions of independence and possible alternative statuses. He also gains something. His first gain is of course the wage, but in addition there are also more subtle benefits—the pleasures of chosen

140

work, of being wanted, of assured status, of participation in a work group, and of accomplishment. All of these items may be large or small or even positive or negative. Similarly, the employer gains something. The product of the work is added to his assets and there are intangibles of power and status. The employer also gives something. Subtracted from his assets are not only the money wages but also something from his personal assets by the responsibilities of power, the uncertainties of the market, and the ulcers that are attributed to the strains of "meeting a payroll."

The problem is that what the employer gives up is not what the worker receives and what the worker gives up is not what the employer receives. Almost at once there is a failure in communication. Each party to the transaction has difficulty in putting himself in the place of the other because this does not constitute a simple imaginary reversal of the exchange. It is a complete change in the significant variables. This is not the case in a simple sale of commodities. When wheat is sold the significance of the money given up by the buyer and the wheat he receives for it cannot be very different from the significance of the wheat given up by the seller and the money he receives for it. The buyers and sellers of wheat are much the same class of people. Class conflict and culture obstacles are non-existant. Parenthetically it should be noted that the exchange between the farmer and the dealer is nearer to the labor relationship and produces somewhat similar sociological consequences.

One more prerogative of the sociologist and the psychologist, not usually thought of as an exchange relationship at all, is the marital relationship. If we speak of a "marriage market" we do so in jest. Nevertheless, it is helpful to organize the study of marriage and the family around the idea of an informal exchange. Each member of the family gains something and gives up something. Many of the communication difficulties arise because that which is given up by one person may not be the gain of another. Hence each individual finds it difficult to imagine himself in the place of the other since, unlike the case of the sellers and buyers of wheat, the experience of one cannot be reversed to create the experience of the other. Indeed, as we examine society, we find that the exchange relationship, as a general concept, is much more pervasive than might at first glance be imagined. Not only in the family but in all social organizations, including the institutions of church and state, a form of exchange relationship is to be found. We give and we take, we take and we give not only the commodities of commerce but also the subtler commodities of the emotions and the spirit—love, trust, respect, confidence, fear, hatred, sorrow, and joy. This is not to suggest that the exchange abstraction is *sufficient* but it is always one useful method of organizing the data.

The study of these *non-commercial* exchanges should lead to a deeper realization of the non-exchange elements in commercial life. As the marital or industrial relationship is more than *just* an exchange, so commercial transactions are not *merely* exchanges. The former involves a subtle environment of mutual respect, trust, and easy communication. The latter can only exist in a framework of roles, statuses, trust, and states of hope and expectation. Without these social-psychological bonds of union the market cannot exist. A group of *purely* economic men would find it impossible to trade! The study of the sociology of the market has been neglected by both economist and sociologist. Here is an area in which the special skills of the other social sciences can be applied to the great advantage of the economist. In other words, the sciences, like nations, should adopt the motto, "Trade, not Aid."

Consider now some possible interactions between economics and political science. Arbitrarily I define political science as the study of the organization of group decision in the presence of conflicting interests and opinions. Thus, we eliminate many of the procedural and legalistic aspects which are of little interest to the economist because they do not fall within the province of his skills. The economist can contribute only where there is *give and take,* wherever there is *negotiation,* either implicit or explicit. Explicit negotiation is the process by which representatives of conflicting standpoints enter into communication to discover a point of view, a statement of policy, or a course of action that will be mutually satisfactory. Implicit negotiation is the process of forming public opinion through the interaction of conflicting points of view in mass com-

143

munication and in personal conversation and interaction.

In a working democracy, for instance, the interaction of political parties should result in mutual *modifications* of the positions of the contending parties in the direction of mutual agreement. Lacking this process democracy will fail. However, this does not mean that the process of *implicit negotiation* has to go on to the point where all parties and all factions stand for exactly the same thing. Nevertheless, there have been periods in the history of many democracies when major parties adopted similar policies and expounded similar philosophies. But, in a dynamic society, new ideas and new points of view will always rise to challenge the old. The equilibrium of universal agreement (toward which the political process works) will always be disturbed by innovators who, in turn, become conservative and are challenged by further innovators in the abrasive processes of political interaction. There is an analogy here to the way in which innovation in economic processes disturbs old equilibria and creates a movement towards new ones.

The political process, as described above, is not always operative. The opposite of the political process (i.e. of negotiation, explicit or implicit) is *war* in the broadest meaning of the term. In war the contending parties do not seek mutually satisfactory points of view but rather unilaterally imposed points of view—in other words, not agreement but conquest. Whenever the process of political interaction results in a *divergence* instead of a *convergence* of points of view the result is likely to be war. This divergent instability fosters the attempts of each party to impose its will on the other. This applies not only to international relations, where war seems to be a normal state of affairs, but also to labor relations and even to family relations.

Economics sheds light on these processes at two main points. The first is in the theory of exchange where we have an instrument enabling us to distinguish carefully between two processes which I have called *trading* and *conflict*. The second is the theory of oligopoly, involving the processes of conflict and warfare.

Unfortunately the full implications of the theory of exchange can hardly be appreciated without following the rather complicated diagrams so familiar to economic theorists and to be found in books on advanced theory. However, the principle is that two different kinds of movements can be distinguished in any field involving exchange. Movements which leave both parties better off may be called *trading*. In exchange, trading takes place when each party receives something worth more to him than that which he gave up. The whole field can then be divided into a set of points at which trading is possible—that is, points from which we can move to positions of greater mutual advantage—*and* a set of points at which trading is no longer possible, that is, from which any movement will mean that at least one party is worse off than before. In a two-dimensional field this set is usually called the *contract curve* although perhaps the term *conflict curve* would be more suitable. As trading proceeds, the possibilities for further trading become exhausted and any process of trading, continued far enough, will end on the conflict curve or at some point where *mutual* advantage is an impossibility.

This analysis leads to some interesting conclusions. The first is that even if we reach a conflict point in one field, trading opportunities may still be open in other dimensions. This might be called the principle of enlarging the agenda—the more dimensions we have the more variables are being negotiated and hence the greater likelihood of finding continual possibilities for trading. This may be observed in labor negotiations where the tendency for the number of clauses in the contract to increase is not unconnected with this desire for more bargaining counters. Frequently, if negotiation reaches an impasse, it is because the institutions or conventions of the situation exclude certain items from the agenda which should be there.

If all the trading possibilities have been exhausted and the parties are on the conflict curve, the only possibility of a non-imposed solution is to establish a process whereby the preference functions of the two parties become more and more alike. In other words, there must be a development of *community* between the contending parties. It must lead to agreement on the best position in the field for both parties together rather than the best position for each party separately. The economist does not have much to say about the processes that lead

146

to a growth of community but he can say something about its nature. In the absence of community, once trading possibilities have been exhausted, there must be conflict. The economist also knows something about conflict, at least in one interesting special case.

In the theory of oligopoly and of competition among the few, economics has been wrestling with the problem of conflict in the area of the market, and some of the conclusions are applicable to conflict in general, especially as it applies to war. Let us assume that two competing firms, located in different places, are selling identical commodities. The firm charging the lower price in any given place gets all the business. If the cost of transportation is to be covered a firm must charge a higher price the further is the customer from the factory. As a generalization this becomes the proposition, *the further the weaker*. In other words, the competitive strength of any organization, whether firm or state, at any spot, is an inverse function of the distance from the home base. Therefore, between any two competing centers there will be a *line of equal strength* along which their relative strengths are equal regardless of whether they are measured by the price of the commodity or the power of their armed forces. Each organization is superior to the other on the home side of the line of equal strength. If one organization increases its relative strength by lowering its factory price or by devoting a larger absolute amount of its resources to armed force, the line of equal strength will be pushed away from the stronger toward the weaker organization and therefore the area dominated by the stronger organization grows at the expense of the weaker. If the strength differential between the two is great enough the weaker organization's area of dominance will be swallowed up by that of the larger. The melancholy history of small firms and small nations is contained in this proposition. The dominant size of organizations in the field depends upon the point at which they run into decreasing *returns to scale*. As long as its returns to scale are on the increase the growing organization will encroach more and more on the weaker. However, increasing returns do not go on forever; eventually expansion will weaken an organization rather than strengthen it. The reasons were examined briefly in Chapter III.

The rise in the size of a firm or a nation is a result of changes in techniques which permit increasing returns to scale for larger and larger sizes of organizations. This is one of the basic principles for the interpretation of human and natural history. Even the relatively primitive techniques of Rome made the city-state impossible in the Roman world. In fact, the city-state only reappeared with the subsequent decline of economic, military, and organizational technology. The invention of gunpowder probably sealed the fate of the city-state forever. Nothing short of a major collapse of civilization could make the city-state viable.

The theory of oligopoly points to some other interesting conclusions with fairly general applications. We know that under certain circumstances competition among the few will lead to the phenomenon known as price warfare. A cut in prices on the part of one firm will push back the boundary of equal strength toward the other firms. Assume there are many customers within the territory between the old and the new boundaries. Also assume that all firms are operating under increasing returns to scale so the gain or loss of customers is a marked benefit or a serious setback. The remaining firms' reaction to the aggression of the first will be to cut their prices in order to push back the boundary of equal strength once again—the position of this line depending on relative prices and not on the absolute price of each firm. This is essentially the same phenomenon as an *arms race* between two nations. Suppose that Nation A feels that the *boundary of indifference,* beyond which it is weaker than rival Nation B is too close to home for safety or national pride. Nation A may then decide to increase its armaments in order to extend the probable boundaries of its dominant area. This however diminishes the dominant area—and hence the security—of Nation B. Nation B will probably retaliate by increasing its armaments to push back the boundary of indifference of Nation A. The latter is now back in the same relative position as before. Increasing its armament still further will only provoke a further response from Nation B. And so goes the arms race until the tension becomes too great and the situation either explodes in war or one party accepts its relative

149

position and refuses to respond to the behavior of the other.

One conclusion of the theory of oligopoly, strikingly relevant to the present world situation, is that the more parties in competition the less likely they are to run into the highly dangerous and unstable race outlined above, regardless of whether it be a price war or an arms race. The threat of one is spread over all the effective competitors and is therefore less likely to provoke responses on the part of any of them. The extreme case is what the economist calls *perfect competition*. This is the situation in which the number of competitors is so large that the effect of an aggressive act by one is dissipated by sheer numbers. It passes unnoticed and provokes no responses. We do not have to go to this extreme, however, before we find a possibility for dynamic stability. Stability, as a lack of response to aggressive action, may be possible in a small group of five to ten competitors. This is simply a matter of each one exhibiting a certain degree of inertia.

The theory of oligopoly thus throws much light on the crisis of the twentieth century. In this century, as contrasted to the last, there are only two autonomous centers of power—a political duopoly. The result is a frightening international instability and intensity of international conflict. The nineteenth century was an age of political *price leadership;* the leader, of course, being Great Britain. In addition, there were enough independent centers of power to make diplomacy (i.e., negotiation, trading for position, and temporary alliances) a practicable alternative to armed conflict for long periods.

The theory of oligopoly also offers some insight into the nature of the *communitizing* process mentioned earlier as an essential characteristic of successful political processes. There is a theorem attributed to Harold Hotelling, sometimes known as Hotelling's Law, which states that when one firm is established in a given location the best place for a competitor to locate is next door or at least as close as possible without being confused with the first firm. This is known as the principle of *minimum differentiation*. It is a corollary of the *boundary of equal strength* principle. If this lies between the two competitors (as it must if competition is to survive) then, as the newcomer moves toward the established firm, it pushes the boundary ahead and so enlarges its market area. It must be careful not to carry the process too far, or the situation will become unstable and neither firm will have protection against destruction by the other. The urge to be near the center of the market brings firms together. The fear of unstable oligopoly, leading to war and the dangers of indefensible positions, tends to drive firms apart. But, if each firm knows exactly what the other is going to do, it will be able to protect itself and hence may risk greater proximity to its rivals. In the opposite direction, however, if there is much uncertainty, firms may forego a good deal of market opportunity in return for the security, real or fancied, which distance implies.

There are implications here for interactions of all

151

kinds. Hotelling, in his original article, calls attention to some applications in the field of non-spatial competition. For instance, under certain circumstances, some products tend to become more alike as each firm seeks to capture as much of the other's market as possible. Hotelling suggests that the convergence of political parties and religious sects is an example of the same principle. The similarity of the Democrats and the Republicans is thus attributed to the desire on the part of each to attract the marginal vote which has no strong attachment to either party and is therefore a contestable area between them. The similarity of the Baptists, Methodists, and Presbyterians may also be attributed to the same principle.

On the other hand, where there is great uncertainty or hostility, we see the reverse. Competition takes the form of wanting to *dominate,* or even exterminate the competitor rather than merely attract customers away. For this reason, genuinely ideological warfare seldom results in the happy convergence of product which, for instance, characterizes the competition in the automobile industry. Fords, Plymouths, and Chevrolets become more and more alike, or even like Cadillacs, but unfortunately the U.S.S.R. does not seem to become more like the U.S.A., or vice versa.

There seems to be a watershed on one side of which there are forces that make for convergence of product and development of a sense of community of interest. On the other side of the watershed there are equally dynamic forces that make for divergence of product, increasing hostility, and oftentimes eventual disruption of the whole system of relationships. The development of the skill capable of moving the divergent systems to the favorable side of the watershed is perhaps one of the most important historical processes. In an age of enormous power it is upon this skill that the ultimate failure or success of the human experiment depends. Power itself is neutral—it can destroy as well as build, damn as well as save, kill as well as heal. Unless the dynamic processes of society lead to the constructive uses of power the more power we have the more easily we destroy ourselves. And, viewed calmly and objectively, it is a very small step over the hill that rises between the valley of destruction and the valley of salvation! Political scientists and economists can do much together to probe the topography of this fateful watershed. Indeed, they must do it if man is to survive.

I am no doubt already pursued by an indignant host of psychologists, sociologists, and political scientists who cry out against my intrusions into their fields. Since one may as well be hung for a sheep as a lamb, I shall continue blithely to the end of my imperialistic forays on behalf of economics. Consequently I invade even the sacred precincts of the natural sciences, or at least the biological sciences, and suggest that economics has something to contribute even here. I would hesitate to claim that *all* systems have some aspects akin to economic systems. I am not sure, as yet at any rate, that economists have much to contribute to the study of nuclear physics. However, as we move toward biological systems we begin to encounter phenomena which show remarkable resemblances to certain aspects of economic systems.

Beginning with ecology, the very name pronounces it a second cousin of economics. The interrelationships of organisms in a forest, a lake, or other environment, so much resemble the interrelationships of organizations in a society that it is difficult to tell who is borrowing ideas or drawing analogies from whom. To say that society is something like a pond alive with interrelated species and organisms is almost the same as saying that the pond can be compared to a society teeming with interrelated industries and organizations. In both cases we have a special case of a general concept—a system of mutually dependent populations. The nature of the populations and the nature of the relationships differ, but one can apply a general theory of the interrelation of populations equally well to either or both systems.

Both the biological and the social systems can be described by a set of n equations with n unknowns. In both systems there is birth (additions to populations), death (subtraction from populations), and growth (excess of births over deaths). The principal difference between the ecological and economic systems lies in the genetic apparatus. Automobiles and beauty parlors are produced by more complex *processes* than horses and butterflies. Usually it requires merely two sexes to

154

reproduce living creatures, but to add an automobile to the economic system requires an immense apparatus of factories, machines, workers, and distributors. The phenomenon of demand is more apparent and more easily studied in economic systems although something like it is never entirely absent in non-human systems. An example is the decline in the numbers of the horse. This is not due to any diminution in potential food supply or in reproductive ability but rather to the establishment of a different degree of *complementarity* between the horse population and the human population as a result of the development of the internal combustion engine.

In Figure 7 we measure the human population of a closed society on the vertical axis and the horse population on the horizontal axis. The line H_0H is the *horse line* showing the equilibrium population of horses for each population of men. Thus, at zero human population, we assume there will be some horses, OH_0; the greater the human population the greater will be the horse population. This is what is meant by *complementarity*. Similarly M_0M is the *men line* showing the human population in equilibrium at each value of the horse population. The point of intersection of these curves, K, is the point of mutual equilibrium of the whole system. We have assumed that men are slightly complementary to horses—that is, the more horses the more men. We now suppose that a technical change— as happened in the invention of the internal combustion

155

engine—*lowers* the horse curve to the position of H_0H' and raises the men curve to M'_0M'. The new position of equilibrium is K', with fewer horses and more men.

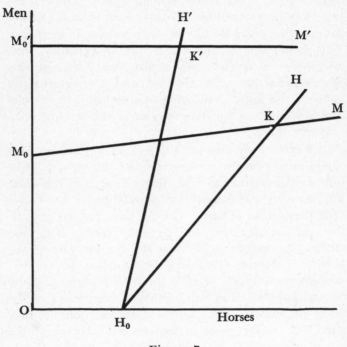

Figure 7.

Something like this clearly happens in nature when the introduction of a new species, or a change in the envir-

156

onment, changes the functions of ecological equilibrium.

We may venture the observation that there are phenomena in the biological world which are also found, and perhaps better understood, in the economic system. An interesting example is the phenomenon of regeneration, found in all living organisms in greater or lesser degree. The starfish grows another arm or the lizard another tail if one is lost, and the worm has the reputation of being able to regenerate both head and tail. In the more complex organisms, the power to regenerate whole limbs and organs may have been lost, but even here, the healing of wounds and the knitting of bones is an essentially regenerative process. We also find a power of functional substitution in most living organisms, that is, if one organ is injured or removed, other organs begin to take over the functions of the damaged or missing one. This property can be observed in as complex an organism as the brain which seems to possess remarkable transfer-of-function powers. This has been demonstrated repeatedly by the recovery of patients who have suffered from serious brain injuries.

I am told that in the fields of biology and physiology these powers of regeneration and substitution are imperfectly understood. We have, oddly enough, a similar phenomenon in economic systems which we understand fairly well. Various industries and organizations of an economic system correspond to different organs of a biological organism and are bound together by the arteries of exchange. They all exist in response to a

157

monetary demand, which it is their function to satisfy, up to the point at which they are normally profitable. Let us suppose one of these industries is eliminated by law—as was the case of the alcoholic beverage industry under prohibition. There will be an unsatisfied demand which will be taken over in part by other industries. However, if the repressive action of the prohibition law is removed through repeal, the liquor industry will grow back quickly to something like its former proportions unless the structure of demand has been changed in the interim. This is the phenomenon of economic regeneration. Economists can reasonably claim to understand this very well through what is called the *price-profit mechanism*. An unsatisfied demand (a function in the system as a whole which is not being performed) will, in a market economy, result in a high price for the product of the function as well as high profits for those who perform it. These high profits attract resources until the growth of the industry lowers profits to the point where further growth is no longer considered profitable.

It seems evident to me that there is value in this model for the biologists and at least they could look for an analogue for *profit* in the cells comprising the biological organism. Without something like profit it is hard to see how there can be anything like regeneration. It does not seem fantastic therefore to suppose there are biological equivalents of the economic concepts of demand, price, and profit and that they need to be identified not only to explain regeneration but also the whole mysterious growth process whereby the genes organize the constitution of living matter.

Economics is neither the queen of the sciences nor the source of all wisdom, but it is a good place to start (though by no means the only one) in an attempt to develop general theories. And there is reason to urge emphatically that all sciences can learn something from other sciences. This process will be the more effective if the autonomy of the various sciences is recognized— especially the social or, as the old Cantabrigian term has it, the moral sciences. It is a well known principle in economics that capital first flows from the more developed to the lesser developed countries of the world but that in time this flow is often reversed. The same can be true of the trade between the sciences, and perhaps in less than a hundred years from now the new world of the social sciences may be able to return, even with interest, the ideological help it has received from the old world of the physical and biological sciences.

The Economic Ethic and the Heroic Ethic

CHAPTER VI

Below the stars, above the mud
Man seeks to find his Highest Good—
He's partly trader, partly hero:
Between infinity and zero,
He occupies a middle place,
One foot in Sin, and one in Grace—

THE STUDY OF ECONOMICS, as well as the skill it develops, does not necessarily result in well defined ethical and philosophical systems, but the pursuit of the discipline does lead the economist to certain predispositions in these fields. Although this is not spoken *ex cathedra* from the chair of economics, my own predispositions in the broader fields of ethics, philosophy, and religion have been profoundly affected by the large amount of time I have devoted to the study of economics. In some sense, therefore, this is a *religio economici*—a confession of that part of my personal faith which has been deeply influenced by my life as an economist.

Adam Smith was a professor of moral philosophy, and most of those in the succeeding generation of economists were ardent utilitarians. Thus the connection between economics and ethics has been a long, if occasionally confused history. The interest of economists in practical affairs has forced them to consider the nature of welfare functions—that is the ordering of alternative situations on a scale of goodness or badness. These welfare functions can clearly relate to organizations or groups. Thus I may judge that A might be better than B as far as my personal enjoyments are concerned but that B might be worse for my family: or that A might be better for my profession but worse for my country: or that A might be better than B for my country but worse for the world at large.

Some of the most difficult dilemmas of human behavior arise from a conflict of welfare functions of different groups. Indeed the attempt to satisfy these dilemmas has given rise to most political institutions as well as to such non-rational adjustments of the human spirit as dogmas and neuroses.

The economist can help clarify these matters. For instance, there is the very important distinction, previously commented upon, between opportunity functions and preference functions. The distinction is important in an ethical discussion because the process that helps to resolve different opinions about opportunity functions is different from the process which helps resolve differences in preferences or value-orderings. Differences over opportunity functions are disagreements about facts, possibilities, or limitations. Consider the question (of some importance in the theory of economic development) of whether the phase of the moon during which a seed is planted, or the amount of fertilizer is more important in determining the yield of crops. The question is limited to the nature of the production function and is capable of resolution by an appeal to experience or to experiment—the latter being merely formalized and controlled experience. In a society in which high yields are desirable it is not necessary to preach the virtues of hybrid corn. Its use spreads because the farmer sees the bushels-per-acre result in his neighbor's fields and is ready at once to imitate a process so clearly and obviously more productive.

In questions involving preference functions agreement is more difficult. The process of establishing agreement, or at least of moving toward agreement, is different and more complex than the process involved in the acceptance or learning of opportunity functions.

The distinction between opportunity and preference functions is simply the old and much discussed distinction between judgments of fact and judgments of value. Some have argued that preference functions or value judgments are not proper subjects for scientific or even quasi-scientific inquiry; that the scientist must confine himself to the safe ground of what *is* (by which of course we always mean what *might be*—that is, the opportunity function) and should not venture into the

162

uncertain quagmire of values where agreement is so hard to get and where *de gustibus non disputandum.*

The economist cannot be content with this counsel of despair. It is precisely the question of tastes (preferences) that characterizes most disputation and most conversation. It is clear that there is a process at work in society whereby tastes and preferences are formed, discussed, and modified. A society in which no such process for the formation of preference functions is taking place cannot really be described as a society at all. The inner integrity of any society must be measured not by the *unanimity* of the preference functions but by the *process of convergence* of preference functions. A society is not necessarily well integrated merely because all its members think alike. Complete conformity may be achieved only by violent suppression of every divergence and thus destroy society's adaptability and capacity for progress. A society in which preferences constantly challenge and modify each other can be one of wide divergences; and yet, as long as a process of convergence is to be observed, that society is healthy. When the processes of interaction do not result in any convergence of preferences or, even worse, when there is actual divergence of preferences, then society is in danger of dissolution—a fair assumption about civilized society today.

What, then, are the conditions under which the process of human interaction produces a healthy convergence of preference functions; and what are the conditions under which that minimum amount of convergence necessary to the stability and health of a society fails to take place? This is not to suggest that an equilibrium of unanimity should ever be reached. The historical process is one of constant and dynamic disturbance with new ideas, new tastes, and new ideals upsetting the old equilibrium, just as innovations constantly upset the movement toward equilibrium in the market. The *adjustments* to innovations must, however, move *toward* and not away from an equilibrium position if society is to remain integrated.

Consider for instance the impact of a disturbing force in the world of values. Such a force is Socialism, challenging the basic preference functions of a bourgeois society. The flexible, loose Protestant cultures of Britain, Scandinavia, and the United States met this challenge successfully by modifications in their own value structure and instituitons. They created what might almost be described as social revolutions in which the *normal* preference functions of society were changed. The revolution was a revolution by consent, by a process of conversation and discussion, by challenge and response.

By contrast the stiff, rigid *orthodox* cultures such as Russia's have tended to break under the challenge, with disastrous consequences for mankind. Indeed the Marxist terminology may be used effectively against the Communists. It is in Communist societies that the dialectical process of history is thwarted by rigid orthodoxy, by violence, and by the suppression of heterodox thought.

164

In seeking to understand those conditions under which convergence, rather than divergence of preference functions takes place, the economist can offer two suggestions in this difficult but desperately important quest. The first is that convergence will be more likely if confusion between opportunity and preference functions can be avoided. A great deal of argument, which in form appears to be about values or preferences, is actually about *fact* or opportunity functions. There is some excuse for this because so many opportunity functions are themselves uncertain. Where real uncertainty exists argument cannot be resolved by simple appeal to the facts of the case. Consider for example some of the discussions of recent years about economic development. Is economic development faster under a regime of orthodox finances, balanced budgets, no inflation, and careful attention to the balance of payments; or does it move forward with greater speed under a regime of unbalanced budgets, uneven development, shortages, imbalance of payments, and constant foreign exchange crises?

This has been part of an argument about an *uncertain* opportunity function. We do not quite know the exact relationships among the various variables of this problem. Moreover, there is really no way of finding out save by a general appeal to history and experience. The problem is clearly much more difficult than that of establishing a production function for a crop. But hidden in the discussion there will inevitably be some argument about preferences. One suspects that the actual decisions that people reach about the nature of uncertain opportunity functions depend not so much on their knowledge of the empirical world as on the nature of their value or preference functions.

Thus, suppose we knew and all agreed about the nature of the opportunity function and suppose we knew beyond all doubt that a little more inflation would give us a little faster rate of economic development. We might then have a legitimate cause for discussion of our preference functions: do we *want* so much more development at the cost of so much more inflation? Here the preference functions of different individuals may well differ and a *political* process of discussion, bargaining, and exhortation must be invoked if agreement is to be reached.

The above illustration is developed graphically in Figure 8. The rate of development is plotted on the vertical axis and the rate of inflation on the horizontal. RMS is the opportunity curve. It is assumed that without inflation there will be some positive rate of development, OR. A little inflation raises the rate of development to a maximum of M, after which more inflation so disorganizes the economy that there is less development as a result.

The preference function of any individual can be expressed as a system of indifference curves. If he does not care at all about inflation but always prefers a higher rate of development to a lower one, his indifference curves will be horizontal straight lines and the

166

preferred point will be M where the rate of development is greatest. If the individual likes development but does not like inflation, the indifference curves will have a positive slope since, in order to compensate the individual for a little more inflation, it would be necessary

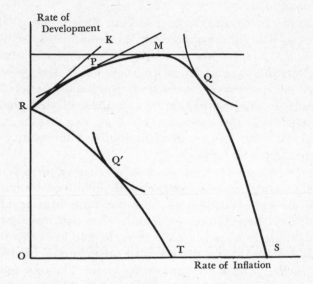

Figure 8.

to have a little more development. The preferred point would then be to the left of the maximum rate of development, say at P. The individual will not go to the maximum rate of development because the amount of inflation involved is judged too costly. And, of course,

167

there might be perverse individuals who positively like inflation whose negatively sloped indifference curves would therefore touch the opportunity line to the right of M, say at Q. This individual would thus be willing to sacrifice a little economic development for the intoxication of inflation.

Let us further assume there is some uncertainty about the exact shape of the opportunity function. Suppose the curve RMS represents an optimistic view of the situation but the facts, as far as we know them, also permit a pessimistic view represented by the curve RT. It is evident that on the pessimistic side the preferred point for all (with the exception of those extravagant admirers of inflation as a good in itself) is the point R, where there is no inflation.

We now assume the case of an individual with very strong feelings against inflation with indifference curves such as RK. Whether we take the optimistic or the pessimistic view of the opportunity function, this individual's preferred point is the same, R, and he is equally satisfied with it. It will be a little surprising if he does not incline toward the pessimistic view. This not only leaves him as well satisfied as the optimistic view but also it gives him a good argument against his opponents. He can point out that on the pessimistic view even those who like inflation a little will not want to have any! On the other hand those who are enthusiastic about inflation will be very much worse off on the pessimistic view of the opportunity function than on the optimistic view. After all, they have to move their preferred position from Q to Q', which is a much less desirable position (i.e., on a much lower indifference curve) on their preference scale. It will be surprising if they do not conceive a certain affection for the optimistic view and even persuade themselves that there is really no uncertainty about the matter at all.

When there is reasonable doubt about the position of the opportunity functions the existence of diverse preference functions will make it more difficult to reach agreement even on the nature of the opportunity functions themselves. Under these conditions individual judgments of value will profoundly affect belief about fact. In so far as science can reduce uncertainty about opportunity functions (this can be regarded as one of the chief practical fruits of the scientific method), it will also assist in the process of convergence of preference functions since the argument will be less confused by disagreements over facts.

As opportunity functions become better known, even diverse preference functions may lead to the same practical result since the preferred point is not affected within broad limits by the nature of the preference function. Thus, with an opportunity function like RT in Figure 8 we see how very wide divergences in preference will still lead to the selection of R as the preferred point. This is not *necessarily* a result of improved knowledge of opportunity functions. In the above case this might lead to the conclusion that RMS was more nearly correct than RT. The diverse preferences would then lead to even more diverse optima. It is not unreasonable to suppose, however, that ignorance leads to undue optimism for, as our knowledge grows, we know more of both what we can not do and what we can do.

The Socialist is likely to be too optimistic about the power of government to do good and the Liberal is too optimistic about the power of the market to prevent evil. A broader knowledge of social science and its iron laws may actually narrow our mental image of what is possible with the result that diverse preference functions may eventually yield the same conclusions. For instance, in the extreme case of complete social determinism, where the opportunity function shrinks to a single point in the n-space of all the variables of society, it is clear that all preference functions will yield the same result. After all, there is no sense arguing about the impossible. No matter what our preference functions, if there is only one point on the opportunity function, that must be the optimum: if there is only one place to go we must all go there whether we like it or no. No amount of scientific knowledge can eliminate the uncertainty and indeterminancy in our overall opportunity functions. There is therefore an irreducible minimum of argument, exhortation, discussion, and mutual conversion.

A problem which is illuminated considerably by this kind of marginal analysis is that of *ethical confusion*. Where the opportunity function and the preference

170

function coincide, or very nearly coincide over a wide area, the position of the preferred point is very sensitive. Quite small changes, either in the opportunity

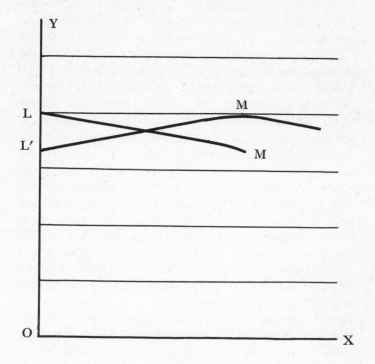

Figure 9.

function or in the preference function, may cause large changes in the preferred position. Suppose (to revert to our previous example) that we dislike inflation and like development. Up to a point, the opportunity function is such that the more inflation there is the more development. Under these circumstances quite small shifts in either function may move our preferred point to the right, to the rigid no-inflation position, or may shift us to the position of being willing to pay for rapid development by quite a lot of inflation. Such a shift is confusing but not necessarily inconsistent with reasonably stable preferences.

An interesting example of such ethical confusion is the constant shift in the Communist Party line. Communists are single-minded people, say, who care for nothing but their own movement toward power, and regard all other variables as merely means to that end. In Figure 9 we represent a variable on the vertical axis which could be called *movement toward power* or the *furthering of revolution*. No matter what variable we place on the horizontal axis—let us say *peace propaganda*—the indifference curves are horizontal. This indicates that the Communist cares nothing for any goal other than the furtherance of his own power. Also, the opportunity functions are likely to be close to the horizontal since there are no strong relations or connections between the Communist's ultimate objective and the subordinate variable. Thus a slight shift in the supposed opportunity function, say from LM to L'M' will shift the preferred position greatly, from L to M'. At one moment then the Communist is all for war, the

172

next for peace; at one moment all for united fronts and the next, all for knifing the Social Democrats.

But an ethical confusion of this kind arises from the Communist's deplorable single-mindedness. He sacrifices friendship, decency, truth, and all other human virtues on the altar of a fanatical interpretation of history. The Communist is not alone in this. Every nation, in the single-minded pursuit of its own security and power, is at one moment an angel feeding the hungry and healing the sick, educating the ignorant and protecting the home; at the next moment a fiend of hell dropping bombs on defenseless people, destroying homes, roasting children, spreading disease, cheating, lying, and indulging in every form of wickedness known to man.

The heart of ethics and of the whole tragedy of man is the process by which preference functions are mutually modified. No matter how we improve our knowledge of the universe and society we are extremely unlikely to reduce the opportunity functions to a single point, or ever to do away with all the uncertainty about *which* consequences follow *what* actions. Preference functions will always be responsible for at least an irreducible minimum of argument, discussion, conversation, exhortation, and mutual conversion. This process is sometimes fruitful and sometimes not. Its fruitfulness may well depend on certain non-rational elements of faith or emotion-centered belief which create a social climate of willingness to make mutual adjustments.

173

In the first place there must be some faith in the *objectivity* of the moral judgment. The question, "What are the *right* things to want?" must have meaning, for otherwise divergent preference systems present no challenge to each other and hence cannot modify each other. A society in which the whim of the individual is supreme in matters of taste and preference would soon lapse into anarchy. This has sometimes been called the "Boo-Hurrah" school of ethical philosophy to whose adherents moral judgment is no more than a purely personal, emotional feeling of approval or disapproval. Clearly, they disprove their position just as soon as they try to make converts.

On the other hand, a very firm belief in the objectivity of one's own particular preference system is also a severe handicap to the dynamic process of convergence of diverse systems. "I beseech you, in the bowels of Christ, think it possible you may be mistaken," wrote Cromwell in despair over the cocksureness of some of his more bigoted followers. Thus when two dogmatisms impinge on one another the result is frequently not convergence of view at all but a sterile withdrawal on the part of each into its own impenetrable intellectual shell.

The recipe for fruitful interaction would seem to be a firm belief in the existence of objective moral truth coupled to an equally firm belief that no one quite knows what the truth is! What is more, there must be mutual respect, consideration, and charity which per-

174

mits *communication*. There must be willingness to listen as well as to speak, to learn as well as to teach, to receive as well as to give. In other words there must be humility. This is of course the reason why the meek generally *do* inherit the earth!

There is an interesting parallel between the conditions I suggest as necessary to a moral synthesis and the conditions which give rise to progress in science. Here too the prerequisite for the increase of knowledge is a certain minimum of faith, hope, and charity: faith in the existence of a stable and reasonable universe; hope that knowledge of it can be increased by careful and objective inquiry; and charity for those who do not happen to agree with one's own views.

The marginal analysis thus throws considerable light on the nature of moral judgment and the ethical problem. The theory of organization discussed in an earlier chapter is equally capable of throwing light on what might be called practical ethics. This is the question of how, in fact, things wrong with the world are, or are not put right. A *wrong* (i.e., something that needs to be put right) is a *divergence* between a perceived ideal and a perceived actual or recorded value of a variable. Therefore, any apparatus or organization directed toward diminishing such a divergence is an instrument of practical ethics.

A servo-mechanism is precisely such an apparatus. If there are wrongs that are not in the process of being righted, it is because there is no adequate servo-mech-

175

anism to correct the divergence between the actual and the ideal. A break-down or a deficiency in any one of the six essential organs of a servo-mechanism is sufficient to prevent its functioning. There may be a defect in the receptor which records and perceives the divergence between the actual and ideal values of a variable. The defect takes one of two forms. One is the failure to perceive the true ideal value and the other is the failure to perceive the actual value.

The ideal value corresponds to the optimum position, i.e., the preferred position on the opportunity function. Our preference, however, may be wrong. It is the function of prophets in society to challenge existing ideals and by a process of argument and exhortation change the perception of the ideal. Slavery is a famous historical example. For thousands of years the institution went unchallenged until a few prophetic individuals perceived that slavery was wrong and eventually persuaded mankind to their point of view. They were able to set in motion the machinery that almost completely eliminated divergence between their perceived ideal number of slaves (zero) and the actual number. As long as this divergence existed it was recorded; the knowledge was transmitted to those who interpreted it as a signal to set in motion all sorts of agitation. Eventually this led to the diminution in the number of slaves towards zero.

When there is historical breakdown in the process of amelioration and when perceived wrongs go unrighted for long periods of time, it is reasonable to look for a deficiency in the servo-mechanism and to devote attention to rectifying the apparatus of amelioration itself.

This might be described as the higher executive function, observable even on the humble level of the firm, where a higher servo-mechanism detects and corrects defects in the lower servo-mechanisms. Thus we may need to devote energy to improving the collection and recording of information about the actual world. A great many failures to correct wrongs merely prove ignorance of the real value of our variables. No matter how efficient the automatic control of a furnace may be, it will fail if the room temperature is recorded by an inaccurate thermometer. The collection and concise expression of social information can well have more important long-run consequences than any other aspect of the past two centuries of technological revolution. The importance of censuses, national income statistics, survey researches, agricultural data, and comparative statistics on national incomes is hard to over-estimate. The collection of agricultural price data led to the dominance of American agricultural policy by the parity concept, and comparative national income data has had a profound effect on international finance and development.

All the information in the world does no good if it does not enter the consciousness of the executive. This is one of the great bottlenecks in the social servo-mechanism. The executives of society—those who set in motion the great effectors and make the great de-

177

cisions—are at the mercy of their information systems. Frequently—and sometimes disastrously—the information they do receive is simply not relevant. Great care should be given to the study of exactly how executives of all kinds—in business, in labor unions, in government, and elsewhere—receive information and how they build images or pictures of their universes from that information.

Also there are frequent serious defects in the effector-mechanisms. The most serious of these is the lack of specificity. We set in motion some action or apparatus with the purpose of changing one variable. Because the action's effect is so widespread, not only is this one variable changed but others also are changed. Some of these latter may be homeostatic and the direction of change may not be the desired one. Attempts to solve one problem may therefore create others, just as attempts to get rid of one evil may intensify many. We wreck the house in trying to swat a fly.

The reader may feel that the economist is presumptious in attempting to deal with questions of right or wrong and good and evil in terms of the apparatus of the marginal analysis and the theory of servo-mechanisms. But one must not under-estimate the power of these devices and it would do no harm for any moral philosopher or even theologians to understand them. Nevertheless, I do not wish to give the impression that all that needs be said on the subject of ethics can be said by means of some simple generalizations from economics. These generalizations are extremely useful in examining the economizing aspects of human behavior: the calculation of benefit, the balancing of gain over loss, and the reasonable assessment of consequences. It must be recognized, nevertheless, that the act of economizing is not morally neutral and that in many systems of valuation it is downright opprobrious.

Depending upon the value given to the act of economizing, ethical principles (i.e., valuation of preference functions) fall sharply into two categories. In what might be called economic ethics the act of economizing is looked upon at least as neutral or even positively good. Then there are a great many systems that might be called romantic ethics in which the cold, calculating type of behavior that counts cost, inquires after reward, seeks to know consequences, assesses probabilities—in short, the behavior of economic man—is looked upon with great disfavor. Much stress is laid on the virtues of impulsive action springing not from the calculation of results but from the inner emotional necessities of the personality. Many diverse ethical systems share the romantic or non-economic element. For example, the military ethic lays great stress on obedience, honor, sensitivity to insult, and willingness to risk pain and death. Surely the romantic opposite of economic man was the senseless *Charge of the Light Brigade* immortalized in English verse by Alfred, Lord Tennyson,

> Theirs not to make reply,
> Theirs not to reason why,
> Theirs but to do and die,
> Into the valley of death
> Rode the six hundred.

179

At the opposite extreme is the ethic of Jesus—a similar insistence on purity of heart rather than the calculation of results, an insistence on love at all costs, on giving away property, on lending without security, on an utter carelessness in regard to the bourgeois virtues. "To give and not to count the cost, to labor and not to ask reward" was the ethic of St. Francis, the most Christ-like of the Christians. This is a far cry from economic man immersed in his accounts of profit and loss.

Nevertheless, one of the great paradoxes of history is that it is precisely the romantic and heroic ethic that is responsible for building empires, founding civilizations, establishing churches, and erecting patterns of culture. In pursuit of romantic ideals men have also destroyed empires, civilizations, churches, and cultures but have proceeded to rebuild them immediately. Economic man goes on through the ages methodically adding up his accounts, equating marginal returns to marginal costs, carrying cargoes here and there, buying and selling, building and storing, ploughing and reaping, creating the physical fabric of society and even a good deal of its spiritual fabric. But no society has ever existed without a religion, even if it be a secular one as in Russia—nor without saints and heroes, martyrs and apostles. It is possible that a society of purely economic men would rapidly reach an equilibrium of stagnation at low level. It would be incapable of producing such essentially romantic and irrational institutions as banks and corporations. It is the visionary —or if you prefer—the crazy man, the neurotic, who creates great enterprises in economic as well as in political, social, and religious life. This is the man who is driven by the repressed fires of his inner volcano, not the man lured by the bait of promised reward. At lower levels of society rewards and incentives, costs and calculations play an important part, but we should be led very far astray in our interpretation of history if we thought that economic man had dominated the scene.

We may say of course that in the long run economics wins; that no matter how much society is characterized by heroism and romanticism, its forms in the long run must be productive or they may not survive. The hero does what he does because it is his nature. Some natures have survival value and some do not. Heroism which tends towards pauperization and suicide needs some counterbalancing element if it is to survive as a culture pattern.

It can be argued that the heroic ethic arises and attains power because of the profound uncertainties of life and opportunity functions. It can be further argued that economic behavior is not possible when applied to the great issues and events of marriage, war, politics, religion and even large business, because the uncertainties of the future make it impossible to balance expected return against cost. Consequently, in the great issues we must act according to our nature and not follow our calculations. We are urged to make great

181

plunges of faith; we must hitch our wagon to a star; we must tempt fortune to the utmost.

Even though heroic or romantic behavior is careless of consequences and is uneconomic in the short run, there will always be a certain natural selection of natures—i.e., types of heroic action—which will cause the more profitable to survive. That is to say there is "profit" somewhere in the heart of the universe; profit in the sense of that profound remark of Jesus, "For what shall it profit a man if he shall gain the whole world and lose his own soul?" The great danger of economic man is precisely that he may lose his own soul, i.e., become a purely "other-directed" person (David Reisman's term), a mere football impelled here and there by the ever-shifting conditions of his environment.

Somewhere in any organization there must be a core of inner integrity, a sense of meaning and purpose and place in the scheme of things. Otherwise the organization cannot survive as a unit of coherent behavior. At some point in the structure there must be inner-direction—a nature or pattern of behavior which is not at the mercy of the vagaries of the external environment. The man or the organization which is "all things to all men" soon becomes nothing to itself.

For these reasons there is a great deal of *complementarity* between the economic and the heroic in the last great production function of the universe; this is to say that attempts to be purely economic or purely heroic are generally unsuccessful. Without the heroic, man has no meaning; without the economic he has no sense. Economic man is most likely to be economic woman— a good wife, pulling the coat tails of her heroic husband, checking his extravagances of speech and action with words of caution and good sense. But without the heroic coat tails to pull, life for both of them would be dull and savorless indeed.

But now, what of the future of man? The reader of the above paragraphs will readily see that I have little sympathy for a purely economic interpretation of history. I am willing to concede great importance to economic and material elements. Perhaps the horse collar abolished slavery, the rudder discovered America, the gold of Spanish America destroyed the Middle Ages; perhaps democracy follows the steam engine, and soils and climate do have something to do with men and their ideologies as well as the crops and stock that flourish because of them. The soft west wind and the peat smoke seem to turn the alien English and Scots who settled in the emerald isle into Irish. The Irish migrate to stern New England and, while remaining Roman Catholics, turn into Puritans. In a generation or two the Japanese in America and the Jews in Israel turn into large, brawny, nordic types. A deficiency of iodine produces defects of the imagination as well as the glands and, as Adam Smith observed, a diet of milk and potatoes seems to produce the most beautiful women and the strongest men. But, when everything has been said on the side of the materialist and the economic determinist, an unexplained residue remains.

Beneath their feet the Indians had immense economic resources and around their heads was the stimulating and presumably invigorating (and intolerable) climate of North America. Yet for thousands of years they scratched but a miserable subsistence from the forest. There is a sharp economic boundary on the homogeneous plain of eastern Europe which divides the high productivity of Germany and the low productivity of Poland. On one side of the line the same soil and climate produces twice the yield of crops produced on the other side. Areas which once supported great civilizations and which are still blessed with the same potential resources have languished for centuries in the grip of poverty-stricken fossil cultures, where those who have the will to advance have no power and those who have the power have no will.

One looks at the broad sweep of human history and perceives only dimly the tangle of loose ends and unfinished purposes. I am more and more impressed with the importance of the non-economic—the heroic, the symbolic, and the religious elements in human life and experience. Economics provides the threads and imposes the limitations, but it is the artist who makes the pattern. If there is indeed, as I believe, a Great Artist and a Great Pattern, it is those in whom the religious sensitivities are most highly developed who are likely to be the most powerful instruments of economic development.

184

The world does not understand this because it is insensitive to these most subtle suggestions of reality as it floats along on the coarse wave of the senses and the sentiments. The bankers and the businessmen, the politicians and the generals, the sophisticated elite, enjoy an illusion of importance. There is a feeling that the world was made for them and they are really determining the course of events. But in reality they are determined; they are the passive instruments of the great iron laws of society, the processes of supply and demand, of ecological equilibrium and succession. These make them or break them, give them meaning for a time and then cast them aside. But the poet, the artist, and the prophet are different. They are the disturbing elements, the destroyers of equilibrium and the ultimate entrepreneurs who unleash the forces of growth within a society.

There have been two really profound changes in the state of man. Some six to eight thousand years ago man was able to hurdle the enormous obstacle separating barbarism from the first civilization. That transition, marked by the domestication of plants and animals and the invention of agriculture, was so great as to stagger the imagination. It is perhaps no accident that the first civilizations—those of Egypt, of Sumer, of Mohenjodaro, and of the Incas and Aztecs—seem to have been theocracies. Reading between the lines of these unwritten histories one can conjecture plausibly that the first great practical arts—agriculture, pottery, and metal working—which created such an extraordinary revolution in the physical and social state of man—were mere by-products of the esoteric inquiries and systems of thought of the early religions.

We are now participating in the second great leap of mankind. It began about the middle of the seventeenth century with the first appearance of science. The first stirrings of the technical revolution in agriculture represents a change as profound as that which led to the first civilizations. The physical and technical equipment of all ancient civilizations were much on a par. Even the great Roman Empire was built on such a scanty agricultural surplus that a relatively slight worsening of the situation was enough to destroy it. As a provider of food the civilized man of 1660 was not very different from his ancestor of five thousand years before.

During the past two hundred years we have witnessed such vast and rapid changes as to dwarf all previous human experience. Imagine a very long-lived Martian astronomer to whom a thousand of our years is but an evening gone. For long periods he has been watching the earth during which there have been no visible changes—even after the appearance of man. For half a million years paleolithic man wandered through the woods without changing them or himself. Ice ages came and went with majestic pace, coast lines shifted, deserts expanded and contracted, but until recently it took a thousand years or more to perceive anything that might be called change on the surface of the earth. Then suddenly, something happened. A few thousand years ago patches of the earth changed color as swamps and forests gave way to fields or as a few dark blotches were made by the first cities. In a rather sporadic manner this phenomenon cropped up here and there over a period of five thousand years. Then our Martian astronomer noticed an almost instantaneous change. On the North American continent the dark forests gave way to the brighter fields and farms and the lines and blotches of roads and cities. The dark stains of the cities grew at a fantastic pace over all the world. The astronomer might well be alarmed as he wonders if this odd planet he is observing is ripening for an explosion!

I am prepared to argue that the scientific and technical revolution through which we are now passing is also, in large part, a by-product of certain non-economic forces. When the creative spirits—the great entrepreneurs of this movement—are identified, we shall find an extraordinary portion of them infected with a sort of prophetic religion and a heroic sensitivity to a truth that counts no cost and seeks no reward. It is not, I think, a mere aberration that Newton was an ardent practicing Christian or that Dalton was a devout Quaker or that such an extraordinary proportion of the great technical innovators of the eighteenth century were pious nonconformists. The method of doubt may be all very well for philosophy, but it is the heroic and imaginative leap of faith which produces both science and technology.

But what of the future? This scientific and technical

revolution—with the end still not in sight—is granting mankind an unprecedented use of power. It may be that this technical revolution is just a flash in the pan, based on the reckless consumption of geological capital in the form of coal, oil, mineral deposits, and even soil. As geologists reckon time, the geological capital of mankind will be used up in a matter of moments. We may face a world in which all mines are exhausted, all minerals and metals dispersed in unavailable diffuseness, where man will revert to scratching a miserable living from the forests in a new and permanent stone age.

The present signs, however, indicate that this view is too gloomy. It is possible that the technological revolution is carrying us beyond the point of increasing economic entropy to the possibility of a permanent high level economy independent of geological capital. It is true that our present system is a high producer of entropy—that is, its operations consist largely in making both energy and materials so diffuse as to be unavailable. Concentrated ores are mined and eventually scattered among millions of rubbish heaps; valuable minerals constantly go down our sewers to become unavailable in the sea; and energy is drilled from its concentration in fields of coal and oil to be dispersed in war and pleasure. But even in this area there are signs of hope. Some of the new technological processes reverse the diffusiveness of the economy. Nitrogen is now concentrated from the air and magnesium from the sea. But utilization of the great permanent source of energy, the sun, still eludes us. It may be that the commercial solution of the problems of photosynthesis is all we need to turn the corner. This alone might deliver us from the spendthrift, consumptive economy of today and release us from the grim law of increasing entropy—at least as long as the sun lasts!

But if these power sources are opened to us—what then? Power in itself is neutral. It can be used for good or ill; and if it is to be used for ill, it is better to be impotent. With the rise in man's power the future, more than ever, rests upon the nature of man's will. If his nature is corrupt—if he wants to do bad things—then the more power he has the quicker he damns himself. This rise in power is largely the result of "heroic" or non-economic forces impinging on man's culture. It is then a question of the right *nature* of the heroic.

There are many varieties of the heroic ethic. Some lead to destruction and some to salvation. I can only conclude, without defense or justification, by offering my own belief. I am convinced that pagan heroism, as represented by Hitler at its worst and by Churchill at its best, can only lead to destruction. All the noblest elements of man are pressed into the service of the pagan state—his courage, his self-sacrifice, and his science. They serve but to accentuate the tragic dynamics of mutual destruction. That man may be saved from his own power I look to another kind of heroism: the heroism of the terrible meek, of those who have seen the vision of perfect, not partial love. I look, that is, to the heroism of the Nazarene.

Alchian, A.A. (p. 61) Uncertainty, evolution and economic theory. *Journal of Political Economy,* 1950, 55, 211.

Barnard, Chester I. (pp. 87, 95) *The Functions of the Executive,* 1938.

Boulding, Kenneth E. (pp. 41, 145) There is much more economics in *Economic Analysis,* third edition, 1955, and *A Reconstruction of Economics,* 1950. The distinction between trading and conflict is derived from *Welfare Economics,* a contribution to *A Survey of Contemporary Economics,* Bernard F. Haley (Ed.), 1952.

Homeostasis (p. 70) For the physiological theory of homeostasis, read *The Wisdom of the Body,* Walter B. Cannon, 1932.

Hotelling, H. H. (p. 151) For "Hotelling's Law" see his article, Stability in Competition. *Economic Journal,* 1929, 39, 41.

Institutionalists (p. 4) The major American institutionalists were Thorstein Veblen, John R. Commons, and Wesley C. Mitchell. The reader will find a highly sympathetic view of institutionalism in Allen G. Gruchy's *Modern Economic Thought,* 1947 and a more critical view in Kenneth E. Boulding's article, A new look at institutionalism. *American Economic Review,* 1957, vol. xlvii, May, 1.

Jevons, W. S. (p. 88) *The Theory of Political Economy,* fourth edition, 1911.

Keynes, J. M. (pp. 4, 5, 22-23, 26, 114) Keynes' two great works were *A Treatise on Money,* 1930 and *The General Theory of Employment, Interest and Money,* 1936. An excellent exposition of the Keynesian system is to be found in L. R. Klein, *The Keynesian Revolution, 1947.* See also Klein's article, A post-mortem on transition prediction of the national product. *Journal of Political Economy,* 1946, 54, August, 286. This is an account of the failure of the Keynesian post-war predictions.

Klein, L. R. (p. 21) *Economic Fluctuations in the United States, 1921-1941,* 1950 and *A Textbook of Econometrics,* 1953.

Leontief, W. W. (p. 21) *The Structure of the American Economy, 1919-1939,* 1951. For a more general discussion of linear programming, see *An Introduction to Linear Programming,* W. W. Cooper, A. Henderson, and A. Charnes, 1953.

Lerner, A. P. (p. 110) *The Economics of Control,* 1944.

Lutz, Friedrich A. and Vera (p. 45) *The Theory of Investment of the Firm,* 1951.

Marshall, Alfred (pp. 19, 21) *The Principles of Economics,* eighth edition, 1920.

Marx, Karl (p. 109) The least painful way to get acquainted with Marx at first hand is to use the Modern Library edition of his works entitled *Capital and Other Writings.*

Mises, Ludwig von (p. 5) *Human Action,* 1949.

Neo-Manchesterians (p. 4) L. von Mises (q.v.), F. A. von Hayek, and Milton Friedman are distinguished members of this school. The essay collection entitled *Collectivist Economic Planning,* F. W. von Hayek (Ed.), 1935, contains some of their best theoretical work.

Nurkse, Ragnar (p. 108) *Problems of Capital Formation in Underdeveloped Countries,* 1953.

Operations Research (p. 64) *Introduction to Operations Research,* C. W. Curchman, R. L. Ackoff, and E. L. Arnoff, 1957.

Riesman, David (p. 182) *The Lonely Crowd,* 1950.

Robbins, Lionel C. (p. 105) *An Essay on the Nature and Significance of Economic Science,* 1932.

Samuelson, Paul A. (p. 27) *Foundations of Economic Analysis,* 1947.

Schumpeter, Joseph A. (p. 13) *Theory of Economic Development,* 1911 in German; Eng. tr., 1934.

Shaw, George Bernard (p. 110) See especially his *The Intelligent Woman's Guide to Socialism and Capitalism,* 1928.

Smith, Adam (pp. 134, 161) The Modern Library edition of *The Wealth of Nations,* Edwin Cannan (Ed.) is the best and most accessible.

Veblen, Thorstein (p. 88) See above under Institutionalists.

Wicksteed, P. H. (p. 21) *The Common Sense of Political Economy,* 1946.

Kenneth Ewart Boulding *was born in England and educated at Oxford. He began his professional career in economics at the University of Edinburgh and later served with the League of Nations. He came to the United States as a Commonwealth Fellow assigned to the University of Chicago and his subsequent academic career included posts at Colgate, Fisk, Iowa State, and McGill Universities.*

In 1949 Mr. Boulding was awarded the John Bates Clark medal of the American Economic Association and later, in 1954-1955, he was a Fellow of the Center for Advanced Study in the Behavioral Sciences at Stanford, California. He is now an American citizen and currently, professor of economics at the University of Michigan.

Mr. Boulding's published works include A Reconstruction of Economics, 1950; The Organizational Revolution, 1953;, Economic Analysis, 3rd ed. rev., 1955; The Image, 1956; *and* Principles of Economic Policy, 1958.

THE TYPOGRAPHY, PRINTING, AND BINDING
OF THIS BOOK WERE EXECUTED BY
JACKSON TYPESETTING COMPANY OF JACKSON, MICHIGAN
CUSHING-MALLOY INC., LITHOGRAPHERS, OF ANN ARBOR
AND WILLIAM B. EERDMANS COMPANY OF GRAND RAPIDS
THE TEXT IS SET IN 10 POINT BASKERVILLE
AND THE HEADINGS IN 18 POINT GARAMOND